THE Path
LIFE TAKES

MICHAEL EARL RIEMER

Interweaving poetry and prose, the author takes us from his youth in the heartland of America through a radically different life in the Philippines. Infused with humor and grace, passion and piety, we are privy to lessons learned through a multifaceted and highly interesting life. Across multiple trials, the unendurable loss of a child, the author's rediscovery and embrace of God, these writings reflect the author's evolving philosophy and deeply felt beliefs. Filled with love and sorrow, triumphs and failures, renewal, redemption, and ultimate fulfillment, this book proves both inspiriting and inspirational.

The Path Life Takes

© 2004, 2018 by Michael Earl Riemer

First edition 2004
First revision 2018

ISBN-13: 978-1-7329061-2-9

Author's email: eldermike547@yahoo.com

Art work by Melissa J. Hoffman

Permission is hereby granted to any church, mission, magazine, newsletter, book, or periodical to reprint or quote from any portion of this book on the conditions that the passage is quoted in context; and due acknowledgement of the source be given. Any portion of this book may be freely distributed, if it is without charge or obligation. The only requirements and qualifications for the above permission are that the name of the author and his email address must be given; and all references from the quoted portion must be provided in full when any portion of this book is quoted.

Unless otherwise indicated, Bible quotations are taken from the King James Version.

CONTENTS

About the Author ix
Preface xi
Preface to First Revision xiii

THE PATH LIFE TAKES (for a special friend). 3
RENEW EVERY DAY (for a discouraged pastor) 4
REFLECTIONS (for a family friend dying of cancer). 5
CONTENTMENT AND PAIN (for a widow with three young boys) . 7
GOING NOWHERE (humor) 8
☙ **JURY DUTY** (humor) 9
TURMOIL AND CHOICE (struggle between the flesh and spirit) . . 12
WATCHFUL EYE (thoughts of God and walking with Him). 13
O THAT (crying out for God) 14
SCATTERED (turmoil and struggle within). 15
THE LOFTY ONE (resurrection of Christ) 17
IMAGINE THAT (humor). 18
☙ **ERUPTIONS OF THE MOUNDS** (a slight malady) 19
WANDERINGS (my struggles and God's answer) 25
AT LAST (realization of God's wisdom) 29
THE TIDE (God's world). 31
PASSING TIME (thinking of the past). 32
CALLING (God speaking to my heart). 34
SHE HAS (for a special friend) 35

THE RIGHT CHOICE (humor)..........................36

ALONE (broken marriage vows)......................37

STATE OF MIND (thoughts on life)..................38

SUNDAY IN THE PARK (time with a friend)...........39

NIGHTMARE (humor).................................40

∽ **I HATE IT WHEN THAT HAPPENS** (a slight difficulty)........41

FIERY TRIAL (confronting challenges)..............45

MY LOVE WON'T CEASE (God's love)..................46

OVER ME (God, the source of strength).............47

DREAMS (thinking of life).........................48

WHAT I SEE (relationship with God)................50

HIS WILL (God's will).............................51

THE SCULPTOR (man's work/God's work)..............52

INTROSPECTION (reflective thoughts)...............54

WHY (unrequited love).............................55

∽ **TWENTY-THREE DAYS** (the life of Hannah Marie Riemer)......58

LITTLE HANNAH MARIE (written during her life).....61

BITTER SWEET REPINE (written after her passing)...65

UNCRUSHED HOPE (beyond the grave).................68

DIRECTION (seeking God's will)....................69

TIME (thoughts on the past year)..................71

SPACE (the Earth, a special planet)...............73

SIXTH BIRTHDAY (daughter's birthday)..............74

TEMPORAL THINGS (fleeting life)...................75

I SEE (victory over the enemy)....................76

SWIFT TIME (reflections on my walk with God)......78

CURRENT BUT NOT CONSUMED (walking in God's light) 80

LIFE (God, the cause and reason for life) 81

INTO THE END (confusion of thoughts) 82

SOMBER HEART (broken marriage vows) 83

THE SEARCH (memoirs) 84

UNBOUNDED SPACE (the universe) 89

SONG OF LIFE (birth to death) 90

SIMPLE PRAYERS (from the heart) 91

FAR AND NEAR (life's journey) 92

THE WEAVER (God's world) 93

THE PRESENT PAST (broken marriage vows) 94

MIND OF THE BEHOLDER (humor) 95

TWO BECOME ONE (a marriage) 97

THINKINGS (humor) 98

THOUGHTS (mulling things over) 99

FORTY SOMETHING (a friend's birthday) 100

CARES OF LIFE BEACON (walking with God) 101

WHEN (marriage commitment) 102

WORDS (the way) 103

CALOMAN BAY (creation days) 104

INNOCENT VOICES (abortion) 106

HERE JUST ONCE MORE (melancholy thoughts) 107

THROUGH A GLASS, DARKLY (recollections) 108

JOURNEY'S END (eternal rest) 124

THOUGHTS ON SELECTED POEMS 125

ABOUT THE AUTHOR

Michael Earl Riemer is a poet, skilled machinist, woodcarver, preacher, home Bible study teacher, Sunday school teacher, and author. Born and raised in Milwaukee, Wisconsin, he now makes his home in the nation of the Philippines on its southernmost island, Mindanao. He resides there with his wife and young son.

He enjoys writing and has authored gospel tracts and articles on various subjects and issues. He has written several books, including *The Path Life Takes*, a collection of poems and short stories; and *Musings on Creation and Evolution*, an assortment of short, well-reasoned arguments refuting evolution. His book *Reindeer Don't Fly* is filled with scientific and logical reasons why the belief in evolution is ill-conceived. *God is One Divine Being* is an engaging study dealing with the Godhead, and his work *ISRAEL, RAPTURE, TRIBULATION: How to Sort Biblical Fact from Theological Fiction* explores the importance of eschatology.

The author's interest in eschatology started shortly before his born-again experience in a Pentecostal church in 1973. It was there that he heard the preaching of an inspiring, "fiery," and well-versed evangelist expounding upon Bible prophecy. The author has been hooked on eschatology ever since.

He is also fascinated by nature and the wonders of creation. For much of his life, he has enjoyed reading about those subjects in books and magazines. But after reading the creation story in Genesis, and the encapsulated history of the earth presented there, and contrasting it against the backdrop of billions of years of evolutionary history demanded by evolutionists and many other so-called scientists, the author began to examine that subject with greater clarity.

With the understanding that evolution is a thinly disguised religion hiding behind the veil of science, he has crafted numerous articles that unmask and expose this dangerous and destructive belief system.

The author is also very concerned about God's Kingdom, our Father's World. He spends some time each week beautifying His Kingdom, by picking up trash, pulling out weeds, and planting bushes and flowers. He teaches those who attend his speaking engagements and Sunday school classes to take dominion over each square inch of ground their feet tread upon, for God is interested in everything—each and every activity done under the sun on His planet, throughout each and every culture and nation.

PREFACE

MANY OF MY POEMS come from deeply disturbing or stressful events in my life. The death of my father, divorce after nineteen years of marriage, loss of old friends, money, home schooling, raising three children, and several unsuccessful business ventures provided any number of stressors. Many things have turned out well, but not exactly as planned. There have been many surprises, some good, some bad.

It seems appropriate that the first poem presented is *The Path Life Takes*. For we are all on a journey that we can plan for, but will probably not turn out the way we thought. Some select feelings and thoughts about what has happened on that path I've put down on paper. I never intended to write poetry. That thought had never entered my mind. And it still amazes me that I had a talent I did not know was there.

Many times in my life I've found it hard to say what needed to be said. But through these poems some of my feelings and thoughts can finally be conveyed. These poems are not just a collection of nice sounding, rhyming words and sentences. They express my feelings and beliefs accurately, but not adequately.

As we travel life's path we experience joy, pain, and many other emotions. Soon the days turn into years, and the baby has now become a teenager. The goals you once had are suddenly out of step with the path you are now on, and you have to change and rearrange your priorities.

The greatest change in my life was becoming a Christian. I would like to report that, now, my friends and coworkers think I am a great and wonderful person—some do, perhaps. But, if you ask them, they would be the first ones to tell you that I am anything but perfect. They would probably say I can be downright stubborn and unthinking at times (they are entitled to their own opinions, even if they are wrong).

But knowing God has helped me to see the greater picture, of how and why events happen in a person's life. Those events change your thoughts forever, along with the actions you take and all else you do and plan to do. It is my hope that the reader may find some encouragement in the fact that others also struggle with life's hard questions. They are not alone; there is a God who cares for and loves them so much that He gave humanity His only begotten Son.

– Michael Earl Riemer
Milwaukee, Wisconsin
December 8, 1997

PREFACE TO FIRST REVISION

There are a few minor changes and corrections in this revision. Five short stories, a few poems, and information concerning the author have been added.

Life has continued on since I concluded my remarks for my anthology back in 1997. I am now a little wiser, somewhat closer to my heavenly reward (maybe very close); and some of life's questions I posed in my poems have been answered. As I continue on my journey to eternity, there have been new events: unexpected turns and unforeseen consequences (not all necessarily bad) from the choices and determinations I had set in motion years ago.

The question I had asked in *The Present Past*: "The union of two, the tie that was bound, now broken and severed, will another be found?" has been answered with a resounding YES! Another precious partner has been found. Twelve years have now gone by since Maribeth and I pledged our sacred vows to honor each other and our God. That union has brought blessings—and unexpected pain and hurt—as you will read about in the story *Twenty –Three Days*.

The question I asked in the poem *Why* has also been answered. All was not as it seemed, for there were a few pivotal factors that were hidden from my view. As the passing of time has revealed, God kept me more than once from much hurt and misery.

Unexpected events, and challenges happen to all, though for God nothing is unknown or unexpected. I have reflected upon the loss of loved ones, the passing away of old friends and family members. I have seen the strength and energy of youth slowly fade the older I grow. As I now ponder the events, joys, trials, and losses I've experienced through the years, that which was unknown has been revealed, and I can see the hand of the Lord guiding my life.

For other events, the reasons are still just as murky as when they first occurred. At times I can't help but wonder *For what purpose was this trial? What was the reason for the death of our child? How do these episodes fit into your plans, your objectives, Lord? How do such challenges advance your Kingdom?* Of course, we all grow old and die, but when your child of just a few days or years goes to meet the Lord before her parents, it is perplexing as to the reason why.

Thankfully, there really is an answer to these questions. There is a reason and a purpose for every occurrence in the life of a Christian, even when that reason may never be known. *"And we know that all things work together for good to them that love God, to them who are the called according to his purpose"* (Romans 8:28).

– MICHAEL EARL RIEMER
*San Francisco,
Agusan Del Sur, Philippines
December 31, 2016*

THE Path
LIFE TAKES

THE PATH LIFE TAKES

A thing of beauty is a wild horse,
As it runs along the way.
It doesn't stop and ponder
All it will do today.

It knows not the sorrow
A broken heart can bring.
It doesn't know the warmth,
The way a loving hug
Can cause your heart to sing.

It feels not the pain
Caused by selfishness and pride.
It does not feel so alone
That it wants to run and hide.

It only knows it likes
To run along the plain.
And it does not stop to worry
'Bout the things in life to gain.

Sometimes I feel I'd like
To be that wild horse.
Just to run along the plain,
And let life take its course.

But if I never had pain,
Heartache, care, or strife,
I'd never know the depths of joy
That God can give to life.

So, though it might be nice
To live carefree like a wild horse,
God can still give great joy,
While problems around you course.

RENEW EVERY DAY

As I came in the door I looked around.
I was disappointed at what I found.
Where were the people to sing and to pray?
It seemed they all just stayed away.

And why am I coming in here today,
When the few that are here don't want to pray?
Am I just beating the air, like Paul had once said?
Am I preaching to those who appear to be dead?

But I must now remember, I must not forget
That God gives the increase, and He's not done yet.
God brings the rain, the storms, and the clouds,
Pain and sorrow His wisdom allows.

God's tender mercies renew every day,
But only if we trust and don't cease to pray.
And what good would it do to plant flowers and trees,
For without clouds and rain they would soon cease to be.

God has a plan we all must construe.
And what God plants and waters is His work, that's true.
So recall Aaron's rod and Ezekiel's dry bones,
Where once there was death, there now life roams.

Great is thy faithfulness.

– Lamentations 3:22-23

REFLECTIONS

Rain on the just and unjust will fall,
And God with His mercy splashes us all.
At times the sunshine will make us feel glad.
At times the rain will not be so bad.

It has rained and poured at times in my life.
And thank God it wasn't all in one night.
Joy and peace were sprinkled like dew.
Heartache and pain were far and few.

The cares of this life at times got me down.
But around every corner new joy did abound.
It wasn't all laughter or sorrow, I'm glad.
There was plenty of both, so I don't feel so bad.

At times in my life I asked, "God, why me?"
He said, "I'm the Good Shepherd,
And that's how it must be.
My mercy and grace are sufficient for thee."

God sees a far through darkness and light.
He knows what is good and He knows what is right.
God crafted the hills, the mountains, and plains.
How He made all, God's Word does explain.

God sees every tear that I cry.
Through children and friends, He wipes them all dry.
With kind words and love the heart heals at last.
With compassion and peace contentment is cast.

The love of God, so wondrous and old,
With wisdom and mercy that cannot be told.
With thoughts high as the heavens above,
He looks down on us all with heavenly love.

I have been young, and now am old, yet have I not seen the righteous forsaken, nor his seed begging bread.

– Psalms 37:25

CONTENTMENT AND PAIN

Some are blessed with fortune and fame.
Others seem cursed with sorrow and shame.
Some are depressed with all they have gained.
Others live lives of contentment with pain.

Death and woe in this life we will see.
Inevitably; that is how it will be.
Why can't we live long like Redwood trees,
Two thousand years and then cease to be?
But would departing this earth be sweeter then,
After so many years without an end?

It is painful at times and I just want to cry.
It is painful, *Oh God, I just want to die.*
Cry if you must, it is not wrong
To cry for things that are now gone.

But God in His wisdom looks down and sees
Places and things that need to be.
Houses and land, pruning, and then,
God tears us down and reforms us again.

Reforms us how we need to be,
Useful for Him and others in need.
Strong you must be for those in your care.
God will help you, your burdens to share.

He is no stranger to grief or to care.
Just call on Him, He will carry you there.
There to a place with God where you'll find
Peace and blessing, for now and all time.

I have learned, in whatsoever state I am, therewith to be content.
– Philippians 4:11

GOING NOWHERE

At times I wonder where I'm going.
I don't know where I've been.
So I'll probably be arriving
Nowhere once again.

I don't remember what I've done.
I don't know what I'll do.
Every careful plan I held
Vanished from my view.

I feel I'm going nowhere fast,
But soon I shall arrive.
It should be much more pleasant
Where I feel I can abide.

My jumbled thoughts are playing
Havoc with my mind.
Here and there, and everywhere,
I'm running out of time.

Twist and straight, love and hate,
Are tearing at my soul.
Pain and pride, walk and stride,
Will never make me whole.

Evil days and prideful ways
Are roaring like the tide.
So now that I've confused you all,
I think I'll run and hide.

JURY DUTY

Jury duty! Ah yes, I remember my last time. I was sitting idly in the jury box with eleven of my peers, when they brought in the defendant. He was accompanied by his liar, shyster… (AKA lawyer). He was wearing a dirty, worn-out, black leather jacket, had gold chains hanging about his neck, and was covered in gang tattoos. His beady, red eyes glared out from behind a curtain of black, greasy hair that hung down over his forehead (the defendant, not the attorney). He really looked guilty, so obviously he was. My immediate thought was why waste a lot of time hearing useless evidence when this beady-eyed guy is guilty. So right away, to help speed things along, I started yelling, "guilty, guilty, guilty!"

This really upset the bailiff, who immediately came in my direction. It also rattled the judge, who was now pounding his gavel like Woody Woodpecker on oak as he shouted, "Order in the court! Order in the court!"

Well, I had just eaten, so why would I order more cuisine? Anyway, along with the bailiff, who was now almost close enough to pounce, two extra-large, menacing-looking sheriff's deputies with night sticks in hand quickly moved in my direction. The bailiff was the first to reach me.

By this time I was standing on top of the jury box railing, screaming, "Off with his head! Off with his head!" With all this excitement the adrenaline was really flowing, which gave me a strength I did not know I possessed. I easily picked up the bailiff, who was just a wisp of a man, and flung him across the courtroom. I guess it is true that the smaller they are the farther they fly. Hopefully, they will replace him with a bigger guy next time.

Unfortunately for the bailiff, the window did not stop his flight (I always thought the windows in courtrooms were bulletproof), and he went right on through. He was probably glad we were on the first floor.

The next thing I knew, all 750 pounds of sheriff's deputies were kneeling on my back with their knees poking out of my chest. My arms were then twisted behind my back like pretzels, and I was subdued. A muzzle—tailor-made for those who speak out of turn in the courtroom—was placed across my face, and a straitjacket that fit firmly in all the right places was found and quickly strapped onto my body. Then, while I was still thrashing about, kicking like a jackass, loudly uttering unintelligible sentences because of the restrictive muzzle (but thinking of words that should not be spoken in front of your mother), they prepared to haul me away.

But before I could be dragged away to face my fate, news of the bedlam at the courthouse had already leaked out, and teams of expressionless news reporters with their camera crews were there to record the whole process for posterity.

I lay sleeping peacefully in the cell they had tossed me into the day before when I felt strong hands grab me and rudely shake me awake. They then shoved me out into the daylight to be sent to a more secure and distant location.

Judging by the large turnout, it seemed that most of Wisconsin's sheriffs' departments, along with a few members of Milwaukee's elite S.W.A.T. team, were there to give their blessings, say their goodbyes, and help expedite my departure. The army reserve was even invited and had brought a few Bradley troop carriers to the event, just in case. I also thought I heard the rumble of an M1 Abrams battle tank, but maybe not. Too bad though, for a short burst from their 50-caliber machine gun would have been a grand gesture and a great final tribute.

I felt honored to have made the top spot on the Fox local news channel that evening, and there was even an honorable mention on the international news scene. However, even though I am now a man of some reputation (and notoriety), I have never been invited back.

TURMOIL AND CHOICE

Oh my dear children, tell me what do you see
When you look at your father, am I who I should be?
Am I loving and kind, thankful and good,
Helpful, friendly, doing all that I should?

I despair when I see the reflection of me;
I'm not what God planned, the man I should be.
Our Heavenly Father knows what I am.
He'd probably like to start over again.

Am I so poor and blind that I just cannot see
All the darkness and woe that lives within me?
It feeds and grows on thoughts that I see,
And no one can kill them, no one but me.

Why has this pit within my life sown
Such despair and shame, so that I now groan,
Alone with my thoughts as deep as the sea,
Restless and troubled still within me?

I'm chained and compassed within and without,
Not quiet and still, but threshing about.
My flesh and spirit seize and fight.
To the death they battle to win the right.

The choice is mine of how it will be,
Evil and shame or blessing for me...
Jesus's power can do anything!
But I have a choice in this one little thing:

Will I pray and repent, trust and obey?
Or will I just flail and walk away?
The battle in my mind goes on and on.
Will I have death or life when it is all done?

WATCHFUL EYE

Stars, rain, ice, and trees are lovely things to see.
I'm so glad I know the God who made each one of these.
He's stronger than the strongest steel ever known to man,
And gentler than the newborn lamb, bleating for its meal.

God alone can place a star way up in the skies.
He also knows and cares each time a child cries.
He's as lovely as the dew that falls each summer morn,
And comely as a fawn that's just been newly born.

God alone can see my thoughts and know just how I feel.
He alone can guide the fowl and give them each a meal.
He made the sea of grass that lies upon the plain.
He made the crystal snow; no flakes are ever the same.

He moves across the Milky Way like children in the sand,
But reaches down and touches me and takes me by the hand.
Though firm, He gently guides my steps along the way.
I'll never know the sinking sand I was carried through today.

The way's been rough and rocky, with trials and some pain.
But times of love and blessing have fallen after rain.
Affliction, care, and pain have humbled me within.
But I will not be broken, more pain may soon begin.

God's paths are hard to learn with proud and stubborn ways.
It would be so much easier to give Him all my days.
Why such trials I've received, I think I now do know.
They came to help me walk the path and ultimately go
To the place He has prepared, because He loves me so.

Behold, he that keepeth Israel shall neither slumber nor sleep.

– Psalms 121:4

O THAT

O that my soul would seek and never rest
Until God dwells inside with peace and thankfulness.
The emptiness is there, so deep and oh so wide
That only God can fill, so come and live inside.

My heart is not at rest like the ever flowing tide,
Which rushes onto shore but never will abide.
Just like a pacing lion penned within steel bars,
My heart is crying out for the God who counts the stars.

As the hart panteth after the water brooks,
so panteth my soul after thee, O God.

– Psalms 42:1

SCATTERED

God from high above looks deep within my soul.
He's been around a while and is worthy of control.
He'd like to take the turmoil that's scattered all within
And cleanse it by His blood and make me whole again.

But the pieces of my life are so twisted and so torn,
So broken and confused, I wish I wasn't born.
But wishing all I want can never make it so.
I live on this cold earth, growing weary and so old.

As I lie awake at night in my lonely, friendless room,
My thoughts and walls whisper tales of darkness and of doom.
My mind is still so troubled, unsettled and so grim,
Sometimes with no thought of God or ever loving Him.

I've wandered aimlessly, not poised but shaking still,
I'm like a tiny leaf swept down a windblown hill.
My mind's all clouded over, I can't see through the haze,
But God's still there to guide me safely through the maze.

As darkness can't abide the coming of the day,
So within my sinful soul the evil cannot stay.
It's tried to drag me down to the dreaded pit below,
But God with His great mercy has caused a fire to grow.

The refining of my soul has now begun again.
But will it bud and flower, changing all the gloom within?
The working of God's mind I cannot fathom still;
It's a mystery I can't solve and probably never will.

But if I can surrender all my dogged will,
Can He lead and guide me safely up the hill.
The hill that leads to a heavenly realm above,
Where God is God alone, and peace is found in perfect love.

Turn thee unto me and have mercy upon me,
for I am desolate and afflicted.
The troubles of my heart are enlarged.
O bring thou me out of my distresses.
Look upon mine affliction and my pain;
and forgive all my sins.

– Psalms 25:16–18

THE LOFTY ONE

He was wounded in the battle, blood flowed from His side.
He never was defeated, but He winced, bent low, and cried.
The price was very great, much glory put aside.
He was also torn and bruised, but joy was still inside.

His shame was oh so great, crushing pain and agony.
Kneeling in the garden, a place called Gethsemane.
Betrayed by a friend, forsaken by the rest;
Assailed by His accusers, He withstood their cruelest test.

Laid inside a tomb, a cold and barren place.
A light was there that darkness just could not erase.
The glory that burst forth that morn so long ago
Has rippled down through time and can rapture any soul.

The high and lofty One, the God of eternity,
Looks down through the ages in thought of you and me.

Worthy is the Lamb that was slain to receive power and riches and wisdom and strength and honor and glory and blessing.

– Revelation 5:12

IMAGINE THAT

It's there in the darkness, the twilight, and dawn.
It creeps in at morning, at noon it's not gone.
It followed me here and there as it does every day.
It crept up on me while I was at play.

I noticed it there as I sat at my desk.
It came in again while I was at rest.
I thought I might try to run far away,
But when I arrived it was there yesterday.

I hopped on my bike and drove in my car,
And then I ran, but not very far.
For there, don't you know, it stood in the way,
I couldn't go over or under that day.

This thing has just tortured me so.
I've explained this all, so now you do know
That my mind's all burned out and ready to go.
Whatever this is, it just bugs me so.
And now, my dear friend, I'll give it to you,
So now it will hound and follow you too!

ERUPTIONS OF THE MOUNDS

I had been very sick for days, but finally, on day nine, there was a light at the end of the tunnel (I prayed that it was not an oncoming train on a single line track). This malady lasted for many days. For a week I was almost totally incapacitated and in a lot of pain. I also lost five more pounds, on top of the fifteen I'd lost during the previous three weeks from working hard beautifying our road and canal. I haven't been this thin since 1968, when the Irish Rovers were singing their pop song titled "The Unicorn." I looked like I could play an extra in a movie about a concentration camp survivor.

On Monday morning, the eighth of April 2013, this most unexpected affliction erupted upon the unseen, almost unreachable portion of my body, my upper middle back. It wasn't there the night before, but now, greeting me on the second day of the week with the rising of the sun, were four small, somewhat painful lumps between my shoulder blades, each no larger than a very small pea.

At first I thought they were large infected zits, pimples with a bit of an attitude. But no, these were their evil relatives, the ones that like to dig a little deeper into your hide and cause you more pain and require much more time to heal—boils. Not only did I never have a boil in my entire life (at least not that I recall…I think I would have remembered) but, when I got this one, what does he do but bring three of his closest companions with him aptly named Mount St. Helens, Mount Pinatubo, and Mount Olympus (you know, Olympus on the planet Mars, the largest volcano in the known universe). Yeah, all four seemed hell-bent on reaching the biggest size possible!

Well, it didn't take them much time before they got to work erupting and growing in size, overtaking and conquering their new territory. By Thursday morning, all the skin between and around each mound was an angry red; swollen and very painful. Also, I felt like I had the flu, with all of its attendant aches and pains. With the customary regimen of hot compresses applied each day, I knew that each boil would soon open and drain its fluid (primarily made up of the bodies of billions of my faithful protectors, my white blood cells). These little guys must have put in a lot of overtime servicing my needs.

On Friday the mounds began to open and drain somewhat, which made things much more painful. Not only did I still have the "flu" with all the accompanying symptoms, but now each spot where the pus was draining was an open, raw, and very painful wound. Each lesion felt like salt had been poured into it, making the whole area seem like it was on fire! The only relief was the hot compresses, but that did not last long, as the fire would quickly start all over again. And my wife, Maribeth, as she dressed the mounds, would say interesting things under her breath, like, "Wow, look at all the pus that came out of that one this time."

By the time the next Monday rolled around, I did not know which side was winning. According to Maribeth, it seemed the mountains were draining more, getting smaller, and healing up. However, my mother-in-law didn't think so and urged me to go to the doctor. I looked at my back with a mirror and there seemed to be some improvement. But the pain, instead of easing, seemed to be heading toward a higher level of discomfort—as if that was possible. So, because of my pain, I agreed with my mother-in-law and went to the doctor. (Sorry, dear!)

The doctor cleaned the affected area and told us no more hot compresses. He gave me a shot in the rear of an antibiotic. He also gave me pain pills, an oral antibiotic, and written instructions for healing my back. I only resort to antibiotics as a last resort. And I have never, for as long as I can remember, taken pain pills. Even when I had my wisdom teeth pulled, I did not take any pills or medicine for pain. But with this, I made an exception. Yeah, I happily took the pain pills.

The shot, oral antibiotic, and pain pills did give me some relief. By Wednesday night the pain was at least bearable, and I felt a little bit of strength returning. But I was still so very tired. The next day, Thursday, was the first time in a week that I had been able to sit down and do something, a little writing. It seemed that this siege was nearly over, though I thought another week or two would probably need to pass before I was fully recovered.

Now, about those pain pills (happy pills) the doc gave me. I think they may have given me a laughing fit. If it's true what they say, that laughter is good medicine, I sure had one heck of a dose.

Monday evening I was on my bed resting, when I heard Maribeth on the phone talking to one of her business partners. They say cute things to each other to help pump up those in their home-based enterprise. I heard her say to the person on the line, "Are you all fired up!?" Well, I thought, "No, I am not fired up! But just ask me about my back. Now *that* is on fire! Man, it's burning hot!"

She was still talking when I interrupted and told her what I was thinking. Well, for some reason when I relayed my thoughts to Maribeth it really hit my funny bone. I started to laugh and could not stop. Luckily, I was standing next to my bed as I fell onto it in a fit of laughter.

Now this laughter was not a few small chuckles, but hard, sidesplitting laughter—the kind when you can't catch your breath. I was laughing so hard I was crying, rolling around on my bed holding my stomach, and every time I thought about what I had said, the uncontrolled laughter would happen again.

Finally, my mind and self-control returned and I could think about what I said and not laugh. But I can truly say, for about half an hour, I was not feeling any pain, for I was laughing too hard to notice. Nowadays I wish that would happen more often. Who cares if people (like your wife) think you've gone mad—with a lighter heart you will sure feel great!

I then had somewhat of a morbid thought: my back seemed like an ideal spot for an infection. Now, if this bane would have settled upon an arm or leg, and septicemia set in with its tattletale red streak, and I could not get it under control, what would be the only option? To prevent the infection from spreading any farther, amputation of the affected limb is often the standard draconian treatment. So that was good news, for no one could amputate my back! But if they could, my, my, what an odd looking fellow I would have been after that procedure.

I had seriously thought about the infection spreading, for one of the boils was right on my spine and the other three were very close. Could this contagion, because of its so close a proximity to my spinal column, spread even farther, perhaps involving the spinal fluid, and do its dirty work there? What would be the results? Ah, questions to ponder while relaxing on a hammock in the shade during the heat of the day.

Well, on the afternoon of day ten, I stopped taking the pain pills. As Maribeth cleaned the affected area in the morning, she said it did look better. And, as the day before, there was some relief from the deep, burning pain that I had suffered for a number of days. Yes, better days were coming. The misery between my shoulder blades had been drained almost totally dry of things to write; soon I could move onto something new. I just hoped the next interesting event in my life would emerge as a pleasant tale, nothing like an unexpected trip to a hospital.

On the morning of day eleven, there was another slight improvement in my health; I just prayed that it would keep progressing. I actually graphed out my progress on a chart, and if my calculations were correct (I was never really good in math), by May of 2019 I would expect to be in fine shape! However, if there was no improvement, you know the alternative: "Dearly beloved, we are gathered here today to pay our final respects...." (I think I will write my own eulogy—that way I will know what lies will be told about me right before they put me in the ground. Yeah, I don't want it said, "He was such a nice man loved by all who knew him." No, I would spice it up a bit. Maybe something like, "He was one of the greatest the world has ever seen, one of the best, one of the most loved....")

On May 8, a full month since the eruptions started, one of the smaller mountains had finally healed. Slight pain and burning continued from the remaining three, but they were healing as well. However, it appeared, when they were fully healed, there would be a large crater or two left to remind me. Yes, my strength was returning and I felt strong as an ox, though half as smart. But it seemed like it would still take at least another few weeks before the mountains were completely healed and gone.

By June 11, 2013, two months after the siege started, three of the boils were all healed up with only one left, which still had a large, thick scab that would shortly come off. This malady sure took a long time to run its course.

Some may ask, is there a spiritual application or dimension to this story? Was there a deep, mystical reason for the pain God allowed me to go through? Because of this experience, did I get closer to God and better understand His nature, His ways, and what He wanted me to do and accomplish? No. The only thing I learned from this episode is that life simply happens, while the sun shines down on the just and unjust. And in which category I reside only God truly knows.

Sickness, pain, death, and heartache are all a part of this sin-cursed natural world. These afflictions befall everyone; no one is spared. Maybe these things help develop empathy for others who go through pain and suffering.

In the life of a Christian there is no secular (i.e., lacking the one true God and true religion) portion to their existence Godliness and undying faith are always there. Everything that happens and is ever accomplished within the life of a Christian—all work, play, or any purposeful time spent—falls within the parameters of His Kingdom, where God in His perfect wisdom, for reasons known only to Him, allows sorrowful events to befall the mortal beings who live on His planet.

Well, was my weeks-long pain meant for evil, was it meant for good, for rebuke, maybe for correction? I do not know. But what I do know for certain is that this reminder of my own mortality sure gave me something interesting to write about.

But now, O LORD, thou art our father; we are the clay, and thou our potter; and we all are the work of thy hand.

– Isaiah 64:8

WANDERINGS

As I've walked along life's path,
It seems I just now found,
Without God's plans and purposes,
I'd just wandered all around.

Wrong courses of action I did take,
Base goals were my desire.
I should have taken all my maps
And thrown them in the fire.

I've seen God take my well-planned schemes
And cast them all away.
I've seen God take my money
And destroy it in a day.

It seems my plans were not
In keeping with His way.
But has the mischief I devised
Been fully put away?

It seems the struggle deep within
Has not yet been resolved
Because my pride and selfishness
Have not been all dissolved.

Is the way of God a mystery,
A puzzle to be solved?
His way is plain, O man,
His word is uninvolved.

His way is true, I'm sure;
His truth is sure and fast.
But with my feeble ways,
My convictions do not last.

They fade as quickly as they come,
And soon they're in the past.
Lying there and mocking me,
I've failed again my task.

In my bitterness I've cried
To God who's always there.
He's never failed to answer
When I've given Him my care.

Then why within my soul
This weakness lying there?
The warring and rebellion
Have made my soul all bare.

The one true God then slowly said,
"My child, listen well.
The fault lies with you,
In me no failure dwells."

"My mind is vast and great,
It sees all yesterdays.
I know all your tomorrows,
Although they're far away."

"I hold within my hand
All power great and small.
Nothing can escape my grasp…
I see a sparrow fall."

"I know the slightest thought
That lies within your breast.
I see the hurt and pain
That causes you unrest."

"I'm beyond the farthest star,
Across uncharted space.
And closer than the breeze
That blows across your face."

"I guide the salmon on its run
Down unto the sea.
And firmly lead him back
From whence he came to be."

"No other one's as wise,
Who can skillfully design
The workings of your mind
Or a majestic, lofty pine."

"You never will unravel
The mysteries that I see.
The howling of a wolf,
The coral in the sea."

"The beating of lofty wings,
The air you cannot see.
The beauty of the autumn,
Each cherry in a tree."

"My son, you never have
Trusted all the way;
You need to fall upon your face
And kneel to me today."

"Repent and consecrate your life
Before it fades away.
Tomorrow never comes,
You only have today."

Whither shall I go from thy spirit? Or whither shall I flee from thy presence? Search me O God and know my heart; try me and know my thoughts. And see if there be any wicked way in me, and lead me in the way everlasting.

– Psalms 139:7, 23

AT LAST

It's taken me so long, but now at last I see,
Without God in my thoughts, all is vanity.
This spinning sphere where foolish people dwell,
The inhabitants here don't fare so very well.
Rambling and rebellion are running through their minds,
The world cannot run fast enough…it's running out of time.

Pride and haughtiness are expressed in many ways.
Knowledge puffeth up; their minds are in a daze.
They think they know what they need to do,
When all they have is emptiness—
When they are finished and all through.

Degrees they have attained, but they're empty and in vain.
Knowledge falsely so called, so there's nothing they have gained.
The beginning of wisdom they've completely failed to see.
They will never know peace or perfect harmony.

Planted by that river is where I long to be,
Where the chaff is blown away and God is all I see.
The counsel of the Lord, please bind it deep in me,
Then let it flow like potent springs deep within the sea.

The sweetest rose of Sharon is calling unto me,
"Come deeper in, my love, I'm all that you will need.
Your sorrow and your tears, please give them all to me.
I'll take them and will plant them; they're useful you will see."

"The lives that bound around you are hurting and in strife,
But I can take and use those tears from each and every life.
A tender plant can't grow in hard and rocky soil,
But even adamant can loosen through prayer and careful toil."

"The shackles will fall off as life begins anew;
New life from death and strife and all that you've been through.
You have to trust in me, you know where I will be:
In your mind and in your heart, when you kneel and pray to me."

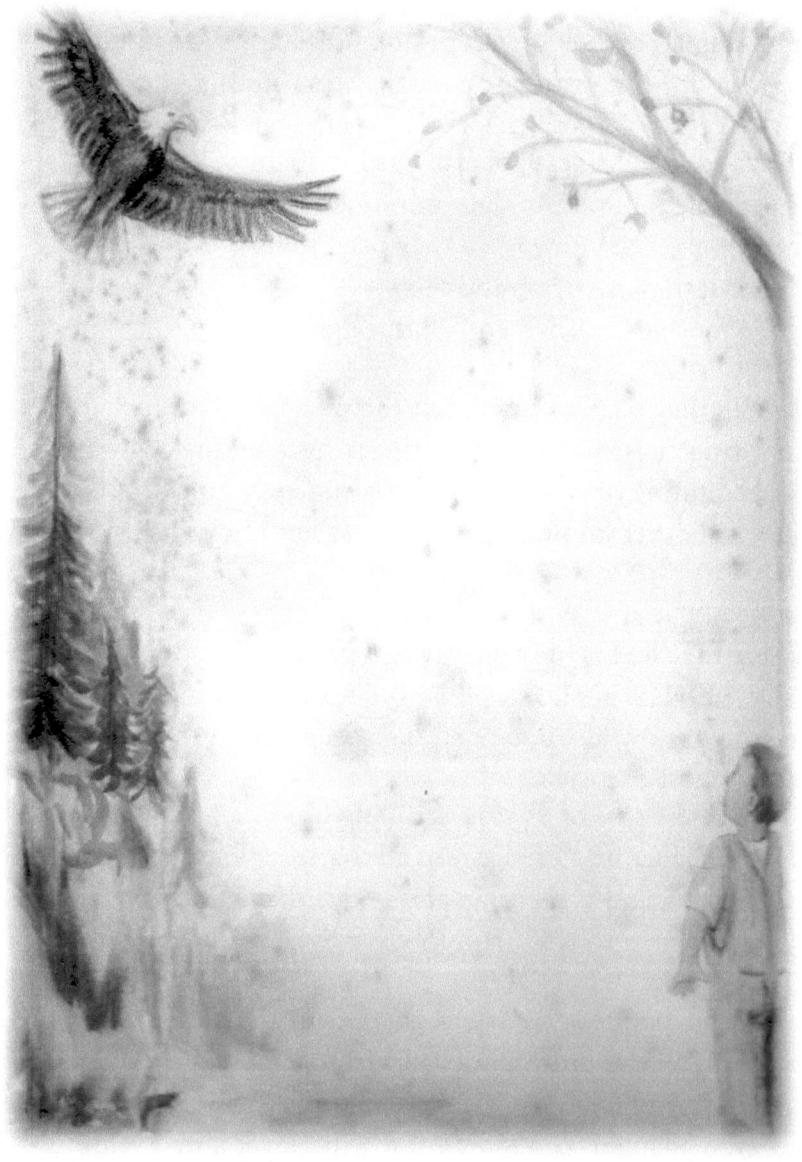

THE TIDE

The swells of tide flood over the shore,
Like pain from deep within.
It churns and dashes up and o'er,
Until it comes no more.

But it's not through, it will be back
To challenge rock and sand.
For with its ever restless ways,
It's something that's been planned.

PASSING TIME

When the cares of this old life abound,
And all your friends have let you down,
And no one hears what you say,
When trials come and seem to stay,
When you're angry with each day,
You want to hide and stay that way.

The face that you now do see,
It's just not what it used to be.
The graying hair, the furrowed brow,
The strength that has left you now.

The years from oh so long ago,
They seem to beckon; they're all aglow
With friends and love, peace and joy,
With fleeting years, they sure seem so.

But things weren't so different then,
It's just your thoughts that may have dimmed.
The joyous times, the happy hours,
Time to stroll and smell the flowers.

The problems of yesteryear
Were also bad you shed a tear.
It's funny how, with passing days,
The bad times seem to melt away.
And any trouble that we had,
Now does not seem all that bad.

If only I could go back when,
I'd surely change events back then.
I'd soon amend every wrong.
I'd do it fast, it would not take long.

But if I changed things back then,
I would not now be where I am.
For only with elapsing time,
Can wisdom grow within your mind.

The knowledge that accumulates
The cares of life necessitate.
That you use what you have learned
Through hard times and love that's spurned.

The prayers that conflicts resonate,
Will not cause God to hesitate.
He'll know just how and what to do.
It will be fine when He's all through.

The past is there, it will not change,
I lack the power to rearrange.
I'm glad I cannot change a thing,
At least I still know how to sing.

The God that is up above
Does not owe us any love.
Along life's path you will find
That all good things will come in time.

Maybe not here below,
But in heaven someday we'll know
Why wisdom takes so long to grow.

CALLING

Knocking, knocking,
Knocking on your door.
Calling, calling,
Calling you once more.

Time, time,
Time is running out.
Will you open now,
Before it is too late?

"Your God is here,
Standing near,
Like many times before."

"I know your mind,
Call one more time,
Send up another prayer."

"Your prayers I've heard, every one,
I remember all you said.
But pray and fast yet today,
For you can't pray when you're dead."

Behold, I stand at the door, and knock.

– Revelation 3:20

SHE HAS

I've thought about these words for such a long, long time,
Flowing here and there, gentle in my mind,
About a special friend I've known for quite a while,
A very lovely lady, precious like a child.

Kneeling in a garden, tending carefully
All the things she's planted and arranged so daintily.
Sitting in a chair, dressed so wonderfully,
Or walking in a mansion, strolling gracefully
Through the rooms and parlors of oak and mahogany.

I see her standing there, thoughtful, full of charm,
Then strolling through a meadow on her thousand-acre farm.
By the ponds and streams, arrayed so skillfully
Her flowing garments trail, rustling prettily.

She'd grace a stately palace, watching o'er the sea,
Or by a humble cottage, kneeling in prayer to Thee.
Her words have meant so much, she'll probably never know
The comfort and the help she has so lovingly bestowed.

THE RIGHT CHOICE

If I had the choice to choose between two,
One or the other, which one would do?
It could be this or that one you see,
For this one is bigger and better for me.

But bigger's not better as I've been told,
So the small one will do that's all yellow and gold.
But I don't like yellow, and gold's not for me,
So I'll take that one, over there by the tree.

But now that I have it here in my hand,
I like it much better, but it's not what I planned.
So I'll put it back just next to the tree.
There, that green and brown one is suited for me.

But what would they say if I kept all three?
Is that selfish and foolish and greedy of me?
My friends and coworkers, what will they say,
When I could choose two, but picked the three?

Now those that I picked are not the right size,
They're big and bulky…just got poked in the eye!
Now I decided what I will do.
I'll forget the whole thing and leave it to you.
But I'm so confused, is it the right thing to do
To leave you the choice—choose one or choose two?

ALONE

How do you feel when it's quiet and still,
And your heart is beating alone?
It's cold and it's bare, she's no longer there,
You're sitting alone in your room.

Your thoughts sit and linger and flounder around,
The daylight has turned into gloom.
The brightness once here is no longer near.
I hear the haunting cry of the Loon.

Its cry slowly glides across the dark sky
And floats up and down past the moon.
It sinks deep inside and then slowly dies,
While my heart plays a slow, mournful tune.

The leaves that have fallen from off of our tree
Float slowly down to the ground.
They're stepped on and crushed, ground into fine dust,
Like the love that once used to be.

Why do the tears still come to my eyes
When I think of what used to be?
That love is now past, I thought it would last
As long as a stately oak tree.

I'll find her one day, I hopefully may,
With joy and hope in her eyes.
This love it will last, until life has passed,
Together forever we'll be.

STATE OF MIND

Gloom and doom, joy and peace
Are opposing states of mind.
They cannot reside, both there inside,
Or how twisted your path it will be.

Your thoughts and your actions all interweave,
Coinciding with what you will be.
You cannot go straight when you're so full of hate.
Only one can win out, you will see.

What you should be, do not leave it to me,
I might have some strange, awful plans.
But God is the one who sent His dear Son
To pardon and purify me.

The turmoil and strife that have ruined your life
Should not plague all you may do.
The mind that's in Christ can bring peace to your life,
So trust Him…He'll give some to you.

SUNDAY IN THE PARK

I thought I'd like to drop a line,
Together on Sunday—it was so fine.
A warm and sunny day,
A charming smile as we walked a way.
I really can't remember when
I didn't want the time to end.

Contentment on the wooded path;
Pleasant lady strolling on the grass.
Again I'd like to see you there;
For just a while I had no care.
For now that time has gone away,
I'd like to do it again someday.

NIGHTMARE

I once had a nightmare, so long ago.
It's all faded and dim, but it won't let me go.
I dreamed the image deep in the night,
It was silent and cold…what a terrible sight.

Its eyes glared at me, how long I don't know.
They were listless and sullen, black just like coal.
It hovered alone in the air like the mist,
Then it shimmied and crawled and flopped like a fish.

It jumped and it rolled around on the floor;
Then it got up and ran through the door.
My eyes were as wide as the moon in the sky.
Next they fell out, and I wanted to cry.

Then my feet, they just started to go
Away after it, why, I don't know.
Fairly soon I caught up with that thing,
Then it sat on the ground and started to sing.

I just could not place the tune that I heard,
But I still can recall every last word.
The song was about a number I called—
'Twas the friendly psychic, they'll tell you all.

The last thing I heard as I hung up the phone,
"Your dreams will be pleasant, there in your home."

I HATE IT WHEN THAT HAPPENS

To promote tourism in the Philippines, the travel agencies here have come up with a slogan: *It's more fun in the Philippines.* Now that might be true at times for some folks, but it was not applicable to me a week ago.

If you would rate, on a scale of 1 to 10, the pleasant things that I have experienced so far this year, the event I relate here would not fall within those parameters. In fact, I am quite sure I would have to rate it somewhere within negative territory, near a minus 15.

Now I like eggs, but not egg-sized lumps that form on my ankle. At times I like to relax in a tub of nice, balmy water, just soaking up the warmth and serenity. But I don't like steeping in water that is home to disease-harboring black slime, fist-sized snails, schools of suspicious and hungry-looking pisces, unpleasant aromas from bloated dog carcasses, or people's trash—including spear-shaped broken bottles and razor-edged tin cans.

It hadn't rained here in over a week, so my newly planted flowers were crying out for a bit of water. Since we live on the second floor, giving all of them a drink was a slight problem. Our apartment building doesn't have an outside faucet or a hook-up for a garden hose, and I didn't want to carry water from the bathroom, through our apartment, and down the very slippery-when-wet tile steps.

I recalled an earlier, unfortunate occasion when the stairs were indeed wet, which caused me to slip and take the express flight down, only ending when I crashed into the closed door at the bottom. The thunderous and abrupt stop left me temporarily unable to walk, so I had to crawl back up the fourteen steps to get to the top. So, not relishing an encore, I had been collecting water with a bucket from our adjacent canal.

After my third descent to retrieve the needed liquid, I climbed the rock wall that lined the canal back to the top with a large pail full of luke-warm, brown-tinted, nutrient-rich water. Regrettably, just as I reached the top I lost my balance and, for a few terrifying moments, went airborne. Luckily, the rocks on the side wall helped to slow my flight by compelling me to bounce and bobble down the entire embankment.

It all happened so fast that, the next thing I remember, I was sitting in the black gunk, slime, and gravel that lined the bottom of the canal. After my hard landing, I sat there in the ankle-deep water, spread-eagle fashion, a little stunned, just wondering how I was going to climb out of this fetid waterway, for I immediately knew my leg and ankle were not in good working order.

I then looked at my leg and the surrounding water for signs of blood, which would have meant I had been cut or speared by something I would surely regret. Fortunately, as far as I could tell, there were no broken bones, severed arteries, or bacteria-laden, sharp pointy objects sticking in me anywhere.

A neighbor saw what happened, and after getting over her shock and amusement in seeing a gringo flailing his arms in a vain attempt to fly, got a young man to help pull me out. Once out of the canal, I put my arm around her shoulder and she helped me limp to our front door, where I sat down to rest and began to watch that day's entertainment, an egg-sized lump that was now rapidly forming on my right ankle.

Yes, sir, I always tell my son Samuel to do a good, complete job on whatever he tackles. This was my way of setting an example, for I managed a complete sprain; the best that old age, natures' gravity, and an implacable rock wall can provide.

A week later, from my knee down, my whole leg was a plethora of blues, purples, yellows, browns, and other colors I had never seen before. I guess it could have been worse: both legs and an arm (or two) could have followed suit and joined the bruise-a-derby already very much in progress.

To help speed the healing process, I began a routine of daily massages on my injured leg and ankle. After a few days I could tell it was helping, for when the masseur twisted and turned my ankle, the decibel level of my screams and moans was down to the roar of a car without exhaust pipes. And the neighbors no longer came out of their homes to see who was being tortured.

This guy was a wonder, for he was able to loosen up my stiff ankle so much that I could swivel my foot around and get my big toe to point to the four cardinal directions while my leg was still stationary. As a result, I was able to get my foot to point in any direction that I wished to travel while my body was pointing in the opposite direction. That did seem a little odd though, for I couldn't do that with my ankle before. But that was really nifty, how I could twist my ankle around, so I am going to have my masseur work on the other foot to get both of them to work crazily in tandem.

Anyway, after three weeks the swelling went down from my toes up; so much so, that the skin on my ankle was no longer stretched tight like an overcooked sausage threatening to burst open. And my right leg was no longer stout like an elephant's, but had slimmed down a bit, closer to the size of a hippo's. If this healing process had continued apace, in a few months I could have done as Mr. Checker suggested—"Let's twist again, like we did last summer."

The saga continues…

A few months after my short flight and quick dip in the canal, the ankle was still a tad painful, but I was thankfully able to walk, run, and generally rely on it.

One night I was sauntering through our dark apartment, thinking, *I don't need the lights on, I live here and know my way around…in the dark…I can do it.* Alas, my left foot, as it moved in the direction I wanted it to go, came in contact with the leg of a chair—a very hard wooden chair with a very unyielding leg—in our living room. Well, it was really just a part of my foot, my toes; not all of them, just the two that habitually reside in the middle, between the other toes. My middle toe, as I bent down in the dark to comfort it, to hold, caress, and embrace it, was now pointing in an entirely different direction then its companions. In fact, it was pointing decidedly to the left, at a right angle to the other toes, like it was signaling a left turn. The other toe was still pointing in the proper direction, but it, too, really hurt.

After a month, my misdirected toe still hurt a bit, but evidently healed in such a way that it looks funny, slightly bent and kind of fat. Now, when I curl my toes, the middle digit does not want to cooperate and remains stiff, unable to bend. I weep, as I realize my toe-modeling days are now over.

If this keeps up, I may never reach my goal of old age, which is always twenty years older than I presently am, with all parts still attached and in good working order!

FIERY TRIAL

A fiery trial, did you ever have one?
Have they cut off a toe, a hand, or a thumb?
Do you still see, hear, run, work, and play?
Do you have a place you can sing and can pray?

Do you have a home that's cozy and warm?
Do you wear clothes that are shabby and torn?
Do you have cupboards that are empty and bare?
Do you have any friends that love you or care?
Have they stripped off your clothes and left you all bare?
Have you no car or any bus fare?

Many trials have we heaped on ourselves.
Many problems will be solved by themselves.
Many a hurt God did not send.
Many a trial the devil's not in.
If only we'd put away all of our sin.

Many trials that cause us such pain
Are because of our sins; we should be ashamed.
Our foolishness, yes, it sure does abound.
Our pride and self-will we should just tamper down.

To pray and repent will help us to see.
Is it really the devil that's after me?
Or is it myself who's chasing me so,
That I'm all tired out, with nowhere to go?

MY LOVE WON'T CEASE

"I heard the prayer, my child,
That you just sent to Me.
My mind and heart are open,
For I still care for thee."

"My hands, My side, My feet
Have scars, don't you see?
I was wounded for your transgressions,
My love won't cease to be."

"My love won't cease to be,
Forever, eternally.
Before the world began,
I loved and thought of thee."

"It's good that you have come
To that place, the end you cannot see.
For now you realize I alone can help,
If you put your trust in Me."

OVER ME

In the ebb and flow of life, sins washed over me.
Like a heavy curtain, they tried to sever me,
From my source of strength, the Holy One I see,
With beams of glory all around, shining over me.

DREAMS

As your dreams go flowing by,
Soon they form a stream.
A stream that's flowing nowhere,
At times it sure may seem.

Sometimes they sink into the ground,
Never to rise again.
Others flow unto the sea,
Where they just as swiftly end.

But resiliency is such
A wondrous human trait.
Your dreams can rise again,
And maybe change your fate.

But being there will never mean
They all will be fulfilled.
Though thinking that they just may be
Can give you quite a thrill.

Thrills are not reality
Or thinking what could be.
But longing and wanting
Should never cease to be.

It's what you yearn and want
That makes it all worthwhile.
Thinking of some good,
You become a little child.

A little child will dream
But not plan away the day.
He doesn't know the future,
He cannot think that way.

The future's not a dream;
It's there, just look and see.
But how it will arrive,
I just cannot foresee.

So knowing not
What shall, will be,
I'll dream it anyway.
For in the passage of my life,
It just may come to me.

WHAT I SEE

What do I see when I look at the sky?
What do I hear when the wind rushes by?
What do I know when I think who am I?

Does God dwell in me when I think of these things?
Is He deep in my heart when I cry and I sing?
Do I count Him a friend, is He rightly my King?

Do I see God in His wisdom and power?
Do I trust Him now and each lonely hour?
Do I talk to Him as I walk in the way?
Do I know the blessings He has sent me today?

Is my mind all at ease when I lie on my bed?
Do my thoughts trouble me, the words I have said?
Is the time that I spend wasted on self?
Have I put God in a box there on a shelf?

The power of God surpasses my needs.
There is wonder and beauty in all of His deeds.
His love and wisdom do not know an end.
His patience and care He does kindly send.

Tired and alone I surely may feel.
But in talking to God, He will kindly reveal
That He alone holds, there in His hand,
The key to this life, do I yet understand?

The fear of the Lord is for every man.
With kindness and love He'll guide by the hand
Around all the snares and pits in the sand.
Then we'll soon see that blessed Promised Land.

HIS WILL

I prayed real hard, and when I was done,
Trials and problems they did come.
So many flowed and rolled over me
I was crushed; I couldn't see.

I was all right before I sought
The power of God, but what He brought!
His great hand enveloped my life,
Though it churned and boiled all into strife.

Tossed and turned here and there
Like clouds of dust, all in the air.
Soon they settled slowly down,
But still no peace I had found.

"The prayer that you just sent to Me,
You said My will you'd like to see.
Then why do you cry and moan
When I bring trials that make you groan?"

"I do love you, don't you see?
I don't afflict willingly.
Like the potter on his wheel,
Fine soft clay will gently yield."

"But you're all marred, hard and dry,
I have to crush to make you cry.
Then again you will see
Peace and joy will flow from Me."

Then I went down to the potter's house.

– Jeremiah 18:3

THE SCULPTOR

Marble from a mountaintop one day was hauled away.
It came before a sculptor who with chisel carved that day.
The form was very rough; you could not see what it would be.
But from the cold, hard stone a figure soon you'd see.

Emerging from that rock, painfully so slow,
A foot and leg and other limbs soon began to grow.
Grotesquely formed at first, hammered blow by blow,
Upon that formless hunk of rock the sculptor's hand moved slow.

The form was growing daily; shortly it would show
The patience and the skill so lovingly bestowed.
His work was now completed, unveiled for all to see
The beauty from the rock, now standing in front of me.

This work he hoped would last much longer than the sea.
But in his mind he knew that that could never be.
Whatever man can make won't last eternally.
Marble, steel, or diamonds, dust again they'll be.

Another kind of sculptor, whose skills surpassed them all,
Was working out some details on a small celestial ball.
He took much hope and care and placed it on the ground,
And lovingly attended each trait that did abound.

But one poor, wretched soul caught His watchful eye.
He'd need to send some rain from His lightning-studded sky.
And so a rough, cold wind was sent across his path.
He'd need to languish in a prison, but that would soon be past.

His love was not full in bloom, a dry spell must soon be.
And from the western sky came heat and humidity.
It seemed to wilt his entire soul, but compassion it did bring.
So because of Thee, all-knowing One, he learned to cry and sing.

Dashed hopes and plans did soon arrive; they came in day by day.
But soon, because of that, he learned to laugh and pray.
Wisdom, grace, and patience must now begin to grow.
And so into his stressful life children then did flow.

Trials, hurts, and problems were sprinkled here and there.
He needed faith and trust…he really had his share.
Mercy, peace, and tenderness you cannot live without.
Hence He sent a lot of grief so those in time would sprout.

Hope and loving kindness were something he would need.
Along came pain and agony, to force him to his knees.
Hardship, pain, and trials were used to change his ways.
The life that now was formed would last eternal days.
The sculptor's work was thus all done; his life was now replete.

INTROSPECTION

The undisclosed thoughts of mine,
In solitude they do repine.
No one else can ever know
Those things on which my thoughts do grow.

Alone within a tangled web,
Reflections there within my head.
Deliberation, meditation,
I'm alone in contemplation.

From here to where do I go now?
Each thought is shown upon my brow
In furrowed lines across my face
That time and hope cannot erase.

WHY

How can God know the end
When I haven't yet begun?
And why's He placed within my soul
Songs that can't be sung?
The fondest dream I've ever known
Will never be fully grown.
It's lying there deep in my heart;
I wish it would have flown.

It grew from such a tiny seed
I never knew was there.
It fills and flows through all my thoughts;
They're pleasant resting there.

I'd give up almost everything
To fill this one desire:
Why can't God just change my thoughts
And douse this raging fire?

Why must I just pine away
These days so long and dark?
Yet as I've wandered all this way,
I've thought about the Lark.
He sings and flies through the air,
As if he has no care.
For God designed the path he takes;
He flies all here and there.

O wise and loving creator God,
I just don't understand.
The sparrow and the bees do go
The way that you have planned.

But we poor, sinful beings
Walk here so carelessly.
We just don't seem to know
Or hear your soothing melody.

The symphony of falling stars
Cascades all through the sky.
They're flashing streaks of light,
Like ribbons sailing by.
The Aurora Borealis,
So wondrous to behold.
And many other beauties
In the heavens are untold.

The planets and the stars
All move in harmony.
The moon and sun, too, follow
Their paths obediently.
But solitary man
Still walks so callously.
Only when we know the Lord
Can we walk gracefully.

Many things about our God
I don't pretend to know.
But the longer I live here on earth,
More questions seem to grow.
I know it's written down somewhere
Your heart you cannot trust.
For if you do, you'll find that you
Will blow away like dust.

Because I'm sure the Lord knows all,
He has answers for my mind.
I know some things He'll never tell,
Some He'll reveal in due time.
The Lord's so much wiser
Than I can hope to be.
I'll just have to trust in Him;
He knows what's best for me.

TWENTY-THREE DAYS

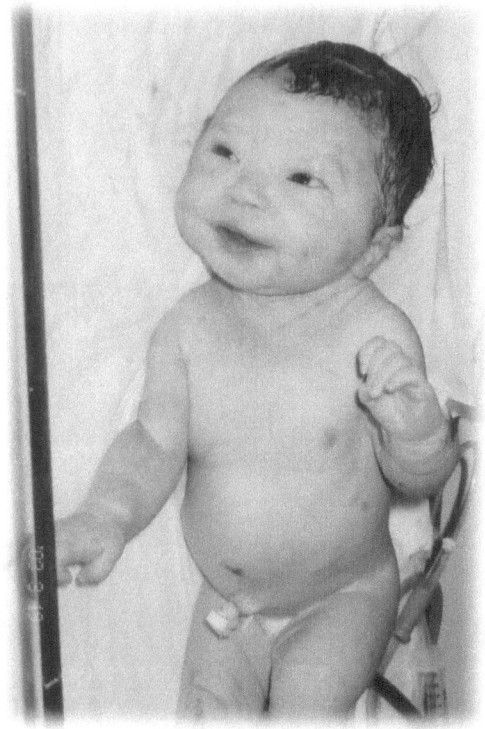

HANNAH MARIE RIEMER
June 15, 2005 – July 7, 2005

Maribeth and I were married in Wisconsin as the summer waned. We had a very limited budget, so the number of guests was small. We found a small wedding chapel that was just right for our nuptial. My wife was young and looked forward to starting a family. Twelve was the number that stuck in her mind as to the correct number of children we should have. She came from a family with six children, so I suppose she thought that doubling that amount would be a good thing.

Two months after our wedding, she announced she was pregnant. It made no difference to us if we were blessed with a boy or a girl; we would have been happy with either. As Maribeth made all the preparations for the arrival of our little one, a few baby showers were thrown for her by our relatives and friends. We were both very excited, for very soon we would have a new addition to our family.

Eleven months after our solemn promise to God and each other, Hannah Marie came into our lives after an uneventful pregnancy and uncomplicated twelve-hour labor and delivery. For her first two hours of life, she was a normal little baby. She was active, she cried, her eyes were open, and she responded to the sound of our voices. She was born with her mother's cute, little button nose; she had long, black wavy hair and brown eyes. A slight smile, such as Mona Lisa wears, seemed to cross her face a time or two. She was eighteen inches long and was six pounds, six ounces of joy and wonderment, just beautiful in every way.

Then, for unknown medical reasons (the autopsy didn't reveal the cause), our baby stopped breathing and suffered what was probably a stroke. This caused severe brain damage, which left her mostly unresponsive with very limited movement and unable to swallow. After her stroke she never cried, nor did she ever open her eyes again. However, after we had spent a lot of time with her, we got to know her. From what little facial expressions and the limited movement she had, we could tell when she was serene, aggravated, or in any discomfort. And when we held her, which was often, we were sure we could see peace and contentment in her face.

The doctors and nurses were always sympathetic and straight-forward about the condition of our daughter, for which we were very grateful. And when I asked them direct medical questions concerning Hannah, they didn't beat around the bush, but always told us the truth, no matter how awful or grim.

A battery of tests were performed, but these only confirmed the doctors' grim prognosis and what I instinctively already knew: that if she did live there was not much hope for any kind of meaningful recovery. I didn't lose sight of the fact that God could fully restore her, but her mother and I knew that God does not always heal, deliver us from our pain and trials, or answer our prayers the way we hoped He would. You may pray, but your loved one may still die. For the most part, God does not perform miracles on our behalf nor change the circumstances; instead, He transforms all who embrace Him. He changes our percep-tions, thoughts, and ways. The miracle He grants us is seen when we suffer loss or pain…it is that deep peace that settles over us, a peace that passes understanding. As the song says, "You can have a song in your heart in the night, after every trial, after every mile…." God gave Maribeth and me that song.

The Bible says there is *"A time to be born, and a time to die…A time to weep, and a time to laugh, and a time to mourn"*

(Ecclesiastes 3:1-4). During the last two weeks of Hannah's life, we wept, at times we laughed, and after her passing we mourned greatly. As the Bible also states, "*It is appointed unto men once to die, but after this the judgment*" (Hebrews 9:27). There is a time ordained for everyone's death, and her mother and I believe that that Thursday afternoon was Hannah's appointed time to be with our Lord.

LITTLE HANNAH MARIE

A blessing came by today;
A little one came to stay.
She brought great joy, but also pain.
Heartache, tears, they still remain.

Long black hair, a little chin.
Tenuous breaths she breathes in.
Her little hand close to mine;
Always in slumber she does repine.

She does not see, lying there,
Her eyelids closed to the cool, still air.
Does she know I am near?
No response from my little dear.

Will she wake and see the day,
The sunset's beauty, smell new-mown hay?
Will she see birds fly
Or see the lightning as it flashes by?

I do not know about these things,
And yet my heart still can sing.
My tears of joy and sorrow flow
Back to God who loves us so.

During Hannah's short life a number of hard decisions needed to be made. But before we made those agonizing choices, we listened to the wisdom of our friends, our pastor, and the doctors and nurses who took care of Hannah as well as other children who had had similar conditions as our little baby.

We constantly sought out God's wisdom and counsel in dealing with Hannah's care. I looked in the Bible but could not find any verses that dealt specifically with our little girl's condition or the kind of medical decisions that needed to be made. There is, however, comfort for those who suffer loss, for the Lord says, *"Come unto me, all ye that labour and are heavy laden, and I will give you rest"* (Matthew 11:28). *"Blessed are they that mourn; for they shall be comforted"* (Matthew 5:4). We truly were comforted.

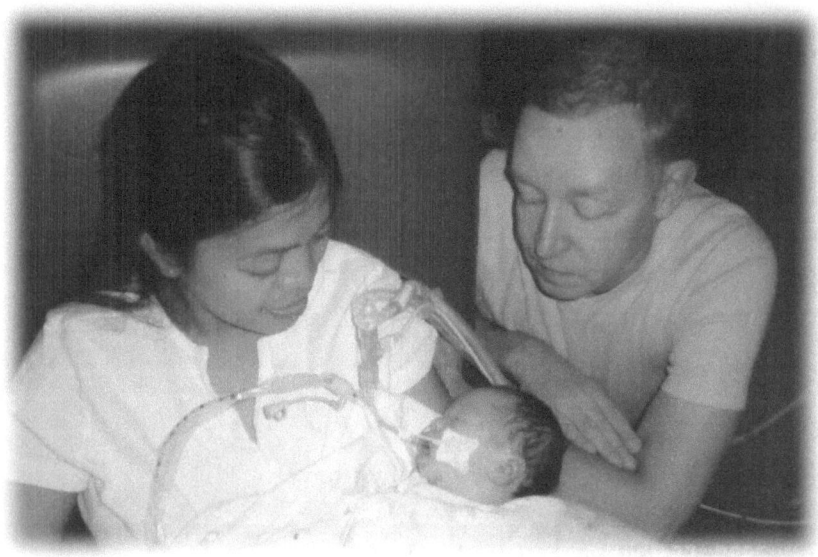

We were glad that the doctors and nurses were so supportive of the decisions we made concerning Hannah's care. Our pastor and friends also supported us in this time of crisis. However, I did hear some criticism of one of the choices we made concerning

Hannah's treatment; some said more medical intervention should have been attempted.

I can state with absolute certainty that neither we, nor anyone else, could have hastened or prolonged Hannah's appointed time to die, even if we wanted to. Our medical decisions—the tough, agonizing choices we had to make—did not thwart God's appointed time for her death. For if you believe in an Almighty God, you should realize that nothing is beyond His control.

Medical science can sustain life for a long time. There is a song that says, "Some say love is holding on, some say letting go…." So how long do you hold on to life? When is the correct time to stop interfering in life's natural course? When is it proper and right to let go? Does it become sinful if a life is held too tightly or for too long? For after her stroke, Hannah would often stop breathing, and would need to be resuscitated on a daily basis. We finally let God determine the answer and placed our daughter's life in His hands. If it was His will for Hannah to live, nothing we did (or didn't do) would make any difference.

We were actually given two very different little babies. One was healthy and the other was severely handicapped. The healthy baby we really did not get to know very well. At nighttime, before she was born, I would put my head on Maribeth's stomach and listen for Hannah's heartbeat; but whether I found it or not, I would talk, read books, and sing to her.

As circumstances would have it, the baby we got to know and fall deeply in love with was not the healthy baby, but the imperfect one—the one who would never walk or talk nor live to see her first birthday. We fervently prayed for her healing, but, shortly before she died, we did not care if God didn't heal her; all we wanted was for her to come home so we could take care of her.

At first, when I realized the severity of my daughter's condition, I felt burdened with all of the extra responsibility that I knew would be required for her care. I really didn't want to tend to such a handicapped little baby. I prayed for God to heal her or let her die. I know it was selfish and unloving, but it was truly the way I

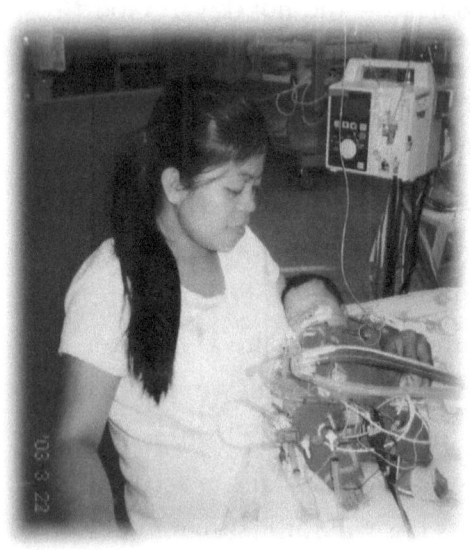

felt. However, as I spent more precious moments with my baby and got to know her, my thoughts and feelings changed so much that, during the last two days we had together, I was finally ready and willing to care for her, and I truly wanted my little Hannah to come home, healed or not.

During our daughter's short life, I watched my wife, who at first was very uncertain of how to take care of her needy little baby, become a mother with all the assuredness needed to shoulder such a profound responsibility. I am very proud of the way Maribeth learned to care for our baby through her 23 days of life.

During the morning of the last day we spent with Hannah, we both really thought she would be coming home in the very near future, for she was breathing very well on her own. But it was not to be.

It was a warm, sunny summer day, late in the afternoon, when she passed away. Shortly after noon, her breathing—which had been steady and strong all morning—began to change to a slower pace. As time passed, Hannah's breathing became more and more difficult. As the interval between each labored breath became longer and longer, we knew she was slipping away. Then came a long sigh, a slight pause, another sigh and slight shudder...and it was over.

God, the Creator of life, received our daughter's spirit. She died enfolded within the loving arms of her mother. I stood near, my arms wrapped tightly around my two precious girls. There was one nurse in the room who was weeping; I, too, was weeping, as was Maribeth.

BITTER SWEET REPINE

Oh, my dear little one,
Your precious life had just begun.
So many days before you lay.
So many joys to come your way.

Your dear ones waited near your side
For your brown eyes to open wide.
So many sights you would see:
The beauty of the autumn tree;
The waves upon the ocean deep;
The memories of this life to keep.

The darkness that held its sway,
We wish you could have torn away.
Our hopes, our plans, our fond desires,
All, my Lord, You did inspire.
The wishes we had yearned to see,
All our hopes would lie in thee.

But now her eyes are closed in death.
Her precious soul with Thee does rest.
Your blessings and your love will hold
Our little one, as time unfolds.

A few days later at the burial there were few in attendance. One of the nurses who attended Hannah at the hospital, a friend, the funeral director, our pastor, and the rain (which seemed the proper conclusion) accompanied us in our sorrow. As the final words were spoken the rain wept gently, as we waited to lay our baby's tiny form in the grave prepared for her small casket...

For a long while after her passing, my wife kept a blanket that had been Hannah's, for our daughter's sweet scent lingered within its threads. At nighttime she would hold it close and dream of our little one; what would have been her first words, what would she look like now, what would be her favorite color, what...what...what?

After her death, God gave us another child, a son whom we love deeply. But Samuel cannot replace our daughter. For parents that suffer the loss of a child, having more children does not heal the hurt felt for the one who now lies within the grave. When your child, so unique, has left this world much too soon, having another can never fill the void. Time does, to a certain extent, lessen the heartache and sense of loss. For a Christian (at least for us), losing a child is a bittersweet sorrow—a sorrow you carry in your memory until you and your child are reunited in the resurrection.

As the years have flown, I do not think about Hannah as often as I did the first year or two after her passing. But during those times when I do look back, I often weep, but not with the inconsolable sorrow of the damned, lost, or heathen; the sorrow I feel is mixed with joy. With the passing of time, my years have increased and become transitory, so I know that soon, very soon, there will be a sweet reunion. I will see my Lord and my loved ones who passed before me one by one, and we will talk and walk with each other under cloudless, sunny skies as eternity passes…with all sorrow, tears, and pain vanished forever.

*And God shall wipe away all tears from their eyes;
and there shall be no more death, neither sorrow,
nor crying, neither shall there be any more pain;
for the former things are passed away.*

– Revelation 21:4

UNCRUSHED HOPE

The only thing there, as you stop for a while,
When you visit the grave of your precious child;
The only thing there was hope for the morrow.
The only things felt were pain, tears, and sorrow.

The feelings expressed before they were gone
Are memories now of loved ones once sown.
With memories faded, now dark and dim,
The love once felt still calls from within.

The one that you seek, now laid in the ground,
You will always remember the love that you found.
As life lingers on, from the depths of your soul,
No words can express, no words can make whole.

The love that still flows down through the years
For the one that's now buried, with hope and with tears
It always will linger inside of your breast,
Kindled at birth, yet not stilled by their death.

But the soul that you seek does not lie in the ground.
Their new life in heaven with God is now found.
The joys that await for those called beyond
Are sorrows now felt by those left behind.

United one day with the souls of the just,
Our hope for the morrow, in God is our trust.
That one bright day our love will entwine
With those gone before, with those left behind.

DIRECTION

I'm thinking of the past from a future point of view.
I'm looking for the future, but the past is still there too.
They change and fold all into one, the present has just flown.
It's ducked and changed into the past, but the future is unknown.

Time and consequence have a hold on me.
And life's many fences corral and bottle thee.
The time for change has now arrived…it's crucial, don't you see.
Unless you're anchored to the shore you'll float on out to sea.

My mind is dull and slow, the wind just wants to blow.
But how and where and will it be, I really just don't know.
Confused about the plan that God has given me;
Overloaded like a fuse, I'm snapped in two and three.

Direction there I see, but will I find my way?
The path of sand where now I stand does not just want to stay.
I've treaded here before, this sand for many days.
Or maybe it was there, the land that's far away.

I've tried to seek with all my heart the High and Holy One.
But with each sun that slowly sets, I've never yet begun.
I need to see the light of Thee, the darkness is all done.
The shadows of the twilight time around me now are hung.

The light of Thee looked in on me, kneeling here below.
But from the corner of my room my prayers don't seem to go.
I just can't seem to consecrate, my mind away does flow
Unto another time or place, wherever seed may grow.

But planted here inside of me's a ray of hope, I know.
For Prince of Peace, Almighty Christ will cause the light to glow.
To shine unto the darkest place, His glory to bestow.
To those who wait upon His name, peace to them will flow.

TIME

Another year's been written down;
It was a time of joy and pain.
My love for God and man
At times did wax and wane.
The time did swiftly fly—
I just cannot recall
Another year so short
It's now a memory, that is all.

The time that I have spent
I cannot hold within my hand.
I cannot place it in a drawer
Or see it on the land.
Did I spend it wisely
For things I cannot hold?
It just has slipped into the past,
It really wasn't gold.

In theory, time, it can't run out.
But when I breathe my last
The time for me will end;
My life will be the past.
But time I have so much,
I just can't count it all.
It flows all through my life
Each summer, winter, fall.

Time can be your friend
Or deadly, evil foe.
Time can go so fast
Or trickle very slow.
Just ask the one in pain,
Dying on the bed,
How much time he'd like to have,
"It was too short,"
He would have said.

But time is never fast
Or slow, it's something you can't see.
For time will run its course until eternity.
Eternity for you is just around the bend
Or maybe many days from now,
But it just as soon will end.

Some things are very costly,
But time you cannot buy.
And no matter how you spend your days,
You soon must say goodbye.
The conclusion of the matter
Was written long ago:
Love the Lord with all your heart,
Your body, and your soul.

For what is your life? It is even a vapour, that appeareth for a little time, and then vanisheth away.

– James 4:14

SPACE

Open space is what I see
As I gaze up heavenly.
Beyond the sky it's dark as night.
No single bird is found in flight.

No whispered sound in that cold realm,
Just emptiness does there abound.
No wee faint voice does emanate
From galaxies way out in space.

No hostile being of flesh and blood
Will ever come from space above.
No comet streaking cross the sky
Can bring strange life to make us cry.

Through God's power, did beings He make.
No strange aliens did He create.
Only angels and Elohim
Are there in space, but can't be seen.

Time and seasons the stars divide.
The moon is close; it brings the tide.
The tide is near twice a day;
It cleans the shore in its own way.

The boundlessness of open space
Shows God's great power, His warm embrace.
Though stars and galaxies do teem,
It's God who fills all in-between.
Only this planet does He encase
With special care and loving grace.

The heavens declare the glory of God, and the firmament sheweth his handywork. – Psalms 19:1

SIXTH BIRTHDAY

Billowed castles towered high,
Backdropped on a purple sky.
Wisps of gold, yellow, gray;
Warm and sun-specked, wondrous day.

June, the middle of the year,
Somewhat older, precious dear.
Golden hair, skipped along,
Eyes that twinkled, sang a song.

Joy, contentment, we did feel;
Sat and played, ate a meal.
Though the time soon ebbed away,
These thoughts within my heart will stay.

TEMPORAL THINGS

Holding on to this old life
Means many sorrows, pain, and strife.
The things that we all hold so dear
Will soon be gone…were they truly hear?

The infinite, eternal maze,
The transient passing of our days.
Our fleeting joy and hope will end.
For what did we, this life did spend?

All hollow things that can't be held
Are shadows that can never meld.
Cascading down around us fell
The muddled dreams where we do dwell.

The fading glow of youth did fly;
It's gone somewhere, unseeing eye.
Unyielding death does grab us tight
Where once we thought we saw the light.

All vain with pride is that short life
Who scorns the one who stills the strife.
When darkness and despair have grown,
We'll know this life we never owned.

The giver of our precious soul
Can walk with us as old we grow.
The boundlessness of His great love
Is majestic, noble, enthroned above.

I SEE

Sheets and sheets of flame
I saw in front of me.
The devil and his minions
Were smiling gleefully.

For I had failed again
The task assigned to me.
A battle I had lost,
Just short of victory.

But the war is still not over,
Many battles yet to wage.
This constant strife and turmoil
Will last me many days.

The Prince of Peace I see.
He beckons unto me.
"Come close to me, my child,
My peace I'll leave with thee."

"Such constant strife and turmoil,
This should never be,
I died at Calvary.
I died to set you free.
I won the victory."

"Your strength will not prevail
For the enemy you can't see.
In darkness he doth lie,
Crouched beneath deceit.
Waiting to spring forth,
To trample beneath his feet."

"All your pride and righteousness
He surely will defeat.
His snares and wickedness
He's practiced a long time.
No matter how long you live,
You cannot match his mind."

"This war you cannot fight
With swords or guns or knives.
But on your knees and with your prayers
You can defeat his lies."

SWIFT TIME

Twenty-five around the Son;
Twenty-five now are done.
A quarter of a century;
Long enough to grow a tree.

The letter that is read of man,
I'm not what I profess I am.
Faithful servant have I been?
Would He say, "come on in"?

So much unseen in the mirror,
Heartaches, tears, all unclear.
Many songs have I sung:
Unbelief, double tongue.

Did I turn some away
Because of my walk one day?
Unstable though I seem to be,
Does He still walk with me?

In the balance I still stand,
Pouring, moving, shifting sand.
Opaque, unknown, dusky way;
The sullen, somber, gloomy fray.

But is it fair what I've said?
Joy's sometimes received instead.
Though clouds may obscure the way,
The sun will shine another day.

Unswerving, constant God is He.
He knows what I'm supposed to be.
Unwaning Master, Sovereign See.
I'll accept what He sends to me.

I am the LORD; I change not.
– Malachi 3:6

CURRENT BUT NOT CONSUMED

Clay or flint, ice or steam,
Solid, soft, not in-between.
How to do and not succumb?
Do I know how to become
The substance He requires?

How to live and not expire?
How to feel and not be numb?
Yield, go, walk, or run,
Eating, fasting, am I done?
Finished what I have become?

Whatever He wants to see,
Tried in obedience I must be.
Life will then flow around
All obstacles that do abound.

LIFE

That mysterious force, the essence of being,
Existence, subsistence, God's power you're seeing.
Your vigor and spirit, the zest and the verve,
A living being means God's somewhere near.

He's upholding, sustaining all things within sight
And things that we don't know that pass in the night.
With power and skill, puissance, and brawn,
God's mercy and love in His beings is shown.

Dirt by itself inert it will be;
Inactive and static, no movement you'll see.
And stones do not grow, a fool you would be
To think that they'll eat or grow into a tree.

A creature deceased, devoid of all life,
Cannot be brought back, will never live twice.
It can't be revived, grows cold just like ice.
Only the power of God can give life.

All wisdom and power and strength to the Lord.
All honor and glory, He gives life by His Word.
All beings does He cause to exist.
Only fools refuse to believe all this.

INTO THE END

Thoughts abound within my head.
The sound of thought is what I said.
Around and through they freely go.
To think of more I was too slow.

Confused, bemused, I sure did grow.
My absent mind like wind did blow.
Though more perplexed, the time still flowed,
A muddled life did slowly grow.

Sufficient though my dreams did seem,
My callused heart into the stream
Washed away all hope, not pride.
My lovely vision of life had died.

Toward the end I now did stare.
Looking back it was all so bare.
All void and shallow, time did show
My flustered life did not go slow.

SOMBER HEART

In the land of mist and gray,
I've thought and pined my time away.
Thinking of another day
When two hearts vowed and knelt to pray.

The solemn words pronounced that day
Were meant to keep, not fade away.
The smiling eyes, the glow now gone,
A somber heart has now been sown.

Some things they say are just not true;
The hurt and pain…it stays with you.
The vows that some so lightly say
Will haunt their dreams some future day.

THE SEARCH

I searched and I sought,
Examined, explored.
I sifted and combed
And pried into more.

I probed and ransacked,
Then frisked and shook down.
But when I did that,
It caused me to frown.

For hunt as I might
And delved into more,
To survey and quest,
And dig up old lore.

It eluded me still,
That rest that I sought.
Distress and disquiet
Were all that it brought.

Belligerent, hostile
At times did I grow.
Serene and tranquil
Evaded me so.

But then, one new day,
The meaning of life
Came unto me,
Brought hope from my strife.

The Ancient of Days,
The Son that was given,
The Prince of Peace,
To Him I was driven.

Gentle and kind,
On wings of a dove,
But also conviction
Was brought from above.

I was changed and renewed,
Cleansed and made whole.
But, still, some old ways
Just refused to go.

At times I'd soar high
And look down from the sky.
But sin still clung
And caught hold of my eye.

Not satisfied yet,
More study did I
With books and with tapes;
They all caught my eye.

Soon a young maiden
Stepped into my days.
Together we planned
Through the mist and the haze.

With a ring and a date,
We both did foresee
Together, forever,
In love we would be.

We romped and we played
And a child we had.
Our diminutive boy
Grew into a lad.

But there, in the darkness,
So cunning and sly;
Waiting to ambush,
With hate in his eye.

That serpent and beast—
I just didn't see
The wicked old sly one,
There waiting for me.

Came trials and problems,
But we did not mind.
Then two more children,
One of each kind.

A few lowly creatures
Walked into our lives,
With long, hairy tails
And sad, lonely eyes.

With joy and delight,
God's word did expound.
To others who searched,
The Savior they found.

Ignoring, not seeing,
The rift in our lives.
The one that I cherished
Started speaking some lies.

The chasm did grow.
How little I knew
The pain and the heartache
That I would go through.

Little foxes, they say,
Will spoil the vine.
And God, in the process,
I left far behind.

My spirit and strength
Carried me through.
But depression and pain
Followed me too.

The God that I knew,
Who could open all doors,
I just didn't knock;
I stayed wounded and sore.

The one that had vowed
To be near to the end
Had now gone away—
No longer a friend.

Belated, prolonged,
Sluggish, and slow;
I finally remembered
Where I should go.

UNBOUNDED SPACE

Far-flung, endless specks of light,
Unbounded, spread throughout the night.
Far-reaching eyes with clear glass lenses
Cull the light the bearers send.

Awe-inspired by their size,
The galaxies, what they comprise!
A trillion flecks of sparkling light
Gleam like crystals in the night.

Twinkling, shining, night and day.
Such beauty time can't take away.
Only man can realize
That God creates these wondrous skies.

SONG OF LIFE

The song of life
We all must sing.
It begins at birth,
Then comes the spring.

The spring is such a lovely time:
Flowers, wind, warm sunshine.
Frost and ice melt away.
Longer days seem here to stay.

Summer now fills our view;
Heat and sun, grass with dew.
Balls and kites fill the air.
Luscious fruit…eat a pear.

Shorter span, the sun does shine.
Yellow, gold, harvest time.
Clear and brisk, moon is bright;
Apple cider, fading light.

Wind and cold sweep away
Crumbled leaves…waning day.
And the joyous song I once sang here
Must now be sung by those so dear.

SIMPLE PRAYERS

Your wisdom, Lord, sent from above,
Is what I clearly need; and acceptance of
My lot below is what I humbly plead.

Forgetting the things that transpired before,
To forgive is the key that closes that door.
A willing mind with love in one's heart
Will heal all the wounds that hate did impart.

FAR AND NEAR

A chasm deep within the earth
I slipped in, fell head first.
Down I tumbled, around did blow.
Is this the bottom or more to go?

Climbing, steep, back to the top.
Finally level, don't want to stop.
Progress to where I need to go;
Far-removed, crawling slow.

Mountain of the Shining One
Where cherubim bow to the Son.
Gates and street await for me.
Repentant, humble, I need to be.

Walking on the fence line.
See the world one more time.
Beckon, calling, swayed again.
The Shepherd says, "I called you friend."

His cloak and garments stained with blood;
His side and hands scarred by love.
The Righteous Judge He soon will be.
But now His love is calling me.

In just a while it will be done.
Like vapor and the setting sun.
Throughout my journey with bended knee,
With heart and soul, I'll cling to Thee.

THE WEAVER

Sun does rise, warms the day.
Clouds the wind does gently sway.
Butterflies wing slowly by;
Birds are flying, bright blue sky.

Thunder rolls, gentle rain,
Waves of grass dance on the plain.
Fertile soil beneath doth lie,
Containing treasures not seen by eye.

Otters frolic in a stream;
Schools of fish swim sight unseen.
Bees and flies go buzzing by;
Ants, they scurry to food that's nigh.

Sun is now a large red ball.
Whip-poor-wills now do call.
Mother doe, with her fawn,
Lay down gently until the dawn.

The weaver of this tapestry
Has more wonders than the eye can see.
The sea and land and sky above
He's made for man, to show His love.

THE PRESENT PAST

Most physical pain stays a short while.
You'll soon heal and mend; it's just a slight trial.
But that ache in your heart, a wound from a friend,
Can it ever be healed, does the pain ever end?

The cutting, sharp words, the deceit, and the guile,
The love you once shared, now broken and vile.
Like a great storm, with its cold, icy blast,
Shadows and thoughts blow in from the past.

The past is still here, though faded and dim.
It cannot be lost; it still knocks to come in.
In and around, through and behind,
Lived all again, just one more time.

It infuses your bones, the joints, and the marrow.
The slightest reminder can give you such sorrow.
You stumble and grope, you don't see the sun shine.
The past's here again, just one more time.

Through blurry, red eyes, the future you see.
But the past clouds it over—seems lonely for me.
The union of two, the tie that was bound,
Now broken and severed…will another be found?

The LORD is good unto them that wait for him, to the soul that seeketh him. It is good that a man should both hope and quietly wait for the salvation of the LORD…For the LORD will not cast off for ever. But though he cause grief, yet will he have compassion according to the multitude of his mercies.

– Lamentations 3:25-32

MIND OF THE BEHOLDER

"What is that?" I did cry.
As it moved and slowly stepped inside.
It was breathing heavy and very deep,
As my eyes from behind my hands did peek.

The floor did shake and I did slide
From one end of the room to the other side.
The walls did buckle and the ceiling quake;
I thought my pounding heart would break.

It slowly turned to look at me.
But it was something I dared not to see.
From there, ten feet above my head,
I saw one eye, which was all red.

Imagine how I did feel:
Soon, I thought, I would be a meal.
I hoped the end would be very quick;
I knew one bite would do the trick.

A terrible roar I could not ignore
Came from the beast I stood before.
With quivering breath I then did plead,
"What do you want, what is your need?"

As I considered what to do,
The floor did sag, and it fell on through.
"Lucky me," I then did sigh,
As I stood at the edge and peered inside.

But is it gone, what I did dread?
The long, swift fall—it must be dead.
But what is that I now do hear;
Something crawling, getting near?

Nigh my ankle I see a claw,
Unblinking eye above its maw.
Four scaly limbs from down below
Pull its bulk, inching slow.

Upward and into the room;
Again I feel close to doom.
Trembling and with ebbing breath,
My deepest fears not put to rest.
The hulking creature before my face;
My greatest fears he does embrace.

Awakened by my rasping scream.
Was it a chilling, foreboding dream?
But, looking now across the floor,
I see a hole not there before.

Fleeting shadows on the walls,
Inky darkness…does death call?
Chilling sounds, my skin does crawl.
Why does this woe upon me fall?

Just in case I took to flight,
Running swiftly through the night.
Thumping, pounding sound, I hear
Something running, almost near?

No more could I continue on.
I have to rest, but is it gone?
Dark creature, do you follow me?
I'll rest beneath this old oak tree.

TWO BECOME ONE

Walking together, the two of us vow.
Working together, we're as one now.
One with the other, unity shared;
Our souls knit together, two hearts that do care.

Two paths no longer, one road we see.
Our life for each other, one flesh we will be.
No longer alone our conflicts to bear.
With help from the other, our burdens we'll share.

The future is far, unseen it will be.
With your hand in mine, we'll walk faithfully.
And when trials come, one prayer there will be.
Because now our hearts beat singly.

THINKINGS

Meditate, ruminate, just in my mind.
Remember, reflection on many a time.
Anticipate, speculate, fancy, contrive.
Imagine, conceive, did it finally arrive?

Deliberation, rumination, reckon, and bind;
Mental absorption, visions in time.
Evaluation, estimation, assumption, and then
I put it aside and do it again.

Consternation, trepidation, apprehension; but when
Comes expiration, termination, culmination, the end?
I guessed and I dreamed, mused and surmised.
But my mind just brooded, while I theorized.

I pondered the thoughts engaged in my head.
My fancy opinions were conjectures instead.
With all this deep thought I just broke a wheel.
Now my mind has to rest; then it can heal.

THOUGHTS

In sunlight and dreams,
There do I see
What illuminates gently,
Reflections in me.

Eyes opened or closed,
At night or by day.
At twilight or dawn,
Reposed or at play.

They're there in the morning,
And all through the day,
Recedes in the evening,
But where do they stay?

The thoughts within me,
What do they know?
Confused and unsure,
They ebb and they flow.

From where do they come,
To where do they go?
Do they cease to exist,
The thoughts that I sow?

FORTY SOMETHING

O, that number I just turned to be.
That four and three's an atrocity.
It cannot be, I was just twenty-three!
How'd that large number sneak up on me?

But a happy thought just popped into my head:
If I just wait a year, I'll be two fours instead.
Still, that's a horrible thought inside of my brain;
The numbers get larger… that drives me insane!

But maybe I'll think for just a slight while;
That number's not large, not really a trial.
Yet to live a long life you have to grow old.
The goal is one hundred, so I've been told.

All of those years that are now in the past
Are my memories…the good ones will last.
And now each new year will add a few more—
As I look back on the past and close each year's door.

CARES OF LIFE BEACON

I know, dear Lord, I've not given my all.
Rebellion just smiles, he's having a ball.
Then pride and lust both jump with glee,
"Don't think about God," they demand of me.

There's plenty of time, here on this earth,
To be born again; to have that new birth,
To walk in the faith of those gone before,
To sacrifice, suffer, to help righteous poor.

I've many long years before that last call.
Although I've been good, am I better than Saul?
But Death might just call, now or next year;
There's no guarantee that he is not near.

So, Lord, send the rain that waters the soil,
And loose my stiff neck with tears and hard toil.
The fallow ground plow with meekness and care,
And for those that are lost, my life with them share.

WHEN

When it's not just ink stains
Dried upon some lines.
Nor a mere, fleeting glance
That holds you for a time.

When words in truth are spoken
And dear as life are held.
When silent thoughts not uttered
Bind long as life does dwell.

And the ring is just a token
Of what lies within the breast.
And honor and character
You can, with trust, now rest.

When the face is like a flint
In righteousness to hold.
When duty to the vow
Will never let you go.

When reversal and calamity
All around you see.
And time and chance transpire,
Your mind unchanged will be.
When unshaken in resolve,
That marriage blessed you'll see.

Whoso findeth a wife findeth a good thing and obtaineth favour of the LORD.

– Proverbs 18:22

WORDS

Uncharted steps of life do flow;
Unending, now, they still do grow.
Unknown by us, but planned above.
Ordered and designed in love.

The words that we, unthinking, say
Are written down day by day.
But mercy and compassion plead;
A repentant heart He then will heed.

So glad that He will not hold
Our hasty words and thoughts untold
Against us when we kneel and pray,
To choose the right and righteous way.

CALOMAN BAY

A long time ago, before the first ray
Of light shown down on Caloman Bay,
The land rose from the depths,
With great power and might.

Creating and molding all things with His hand,
That day was all finished just like He had planned.
Majestic and proud, peaceful and still,
The view of the bay from there on the hill.

Little is known of what was begun,
The time and the reasons before the first sun.
Before the first cloud obscured the bright day,
No arthropods crawled, no creatures did play.
No fowl did call nor horses bray,
The wind just blew across the blue bay.

The vastness of sky did nothing possess.
The waves of the sea—all emptiness.
And silence reigned across a great plain;
No flowers bloomed, no clouds brought the rain.

Blessed to have seen what then transpired,
The forest and jungle now there to inspire.
And flowers with shades of gold and of blue,
Of yellow, of red, and bright purple hue.
Blossoms of white formed then in the trees,
Fruit then did grow amongst all the leaves.

With carpets of green upon all the hills,
And lilacs and lilies by the rocks and the rills.
Abundant the life that swam in the seas,
That flew through the skies, that perched in the trees.
Life that breathed, that walked and had knees,
Praised their Creator from the land, skies, and seas.

The Creator Himself knelt there on the land,
With a handful of dirt made He the first man.
Adam was formed right out of the ground,
But no suitable helper for Adam was found.

From Adam's side Eve was then formed,
His beautiful bride with love was adorned.
Clothed with the rapture of God from above,
The two of them walked enveloped in love.

As the Lord looked down on Caloman Bay,
He was pleased with the life He created that day.
For all was at peace there by the sea,
And love reigned o'er all the Creator could see.

INNOCENT VOICES

Author Unknown

God's wrath is stored up for those who scorn
And consider as worthless the tiny preborn.
These little beings are precious to Him;
He loves and watches the growth of each limb.
And each little baby, imperfect ones, too,
Is special to God, though hidden from view.

At judgment, someday, small voices will cry,
Indicting their mothers who caused them to die.
Accusing the doctors who ended their lives
With suction, saline, with drugs and with knives.

Like Abel, whose blood cried to God against Cain,
Their blood will expose those who caused them such pain.
Then she who once shouted, "My body's my own!"
Will stand mutely in facing her sentence alone.
No longer proclaiming her right to free choice,
But haunted in hell by that innocent voice.

I will praise thee; for I am fearfully and wonderfully made; marvelous are thy works; and that my soul knoweth right well.

– Psalms 139:14

HERE JUST ONCE MORE

I came to the place I came to before.
I came here before; now I've come here once more.
Once more I recall that I've seen it all.
But all that I've seen, I just can't recall.

Oh, but my mind, it just did reel
Because of the way it all made me feel.
But to feel just like this is not so bad.
And if I hadn't been here, I might have been sad.

But here where I am, and where I might be,
I don't understand…it perplexifies me.
But I see all the things I saw here before.
And I don't want to see them all anymore.

But now that I'm done, I'll just walk away.
And now I'm all finished, being here for the day.
But I will be back, just once in a while,
To maybe recall that here I can smile.

I thought the last line was finished and fine.
But my pen was not done, it wrote one more time.
It wrote it all down, and the ink is all dry.
And now as I quit, I'll breathe a last sigh.

THROUGH A GLASS, DARKLY

Marlene Norma (Katona) Riemer
September 22, 1932—August 26, 2013

Robert C. Riemer
June 5, 1928—January 26, 1995

All my memories of mom may not be historically accurate, for some of these events happened so long ago. But here are some of the reminiscences, the recollections I have of mother and my youth. These are probably not the most important incidents in the life of our family, for the mind at times is very capricious and undiscerning of the memories it keeps and what it allows to slip away. Some good episodes (and some not so pleasant) I cannot recall. What follows are a few precious memories that have stuck in my mind and are the way I remember them. Of course, certain details are now some-what fuzzy and are only seen *"through a glass darkly"* (Corinthians 13:12). Nevertheless, my recreation of events is as accurate as I can make them.

Situated on the southwest shore of Lake Michigan is the port city of Milwaukee, where our family made its home. Lake Michigan covers an area of 22,000 square miles, making it the fifth largest freshwater lake in the world. It is one of the five interconnected

Great Lakes, which together, contain the largest volume of freshwater in the world. Residing in our city and its surrounding municipalities, about a million people made their homes.

Our home was in one of the many new subdivisions being constructed in the rapidly expanding northwest quadrant. We lived on West Bender Avenue, an unpaved gravel road. These were the days before the all-knowing environmentalists and their crony bureaucrats began to run amuck, enacting many useless and costly restrictive regulations for our "protection." However, they did put a stop to at least one harmful practice: a number of times during each summer a tanker would roam our neighborhood and spray used oil on the roads to help keep the dust down.

Our modest three-bedroom, ranch-style home was new construction, built on land that had been farmers' fields a few years before. The old provincial farm house is still there, but gone is the small algae-covered, tadpole-choked backyard pond once shaded by centuries-old willow trees. And on its fertile acres of formerly plowed land, where corn and wheat crops used to flourish, there are now parking lots, a park, a freeway, houses, and apartment buildings.

Within a ten-minute drive from our house there was a livery stable where you could buy a saddle or ride a horse for a modest fee. There were also farms where you could pick strawberries in late spring, other produce during the summer, and orchards full of ripe apples during the autumn.

Milwaukee's courthouse, well-regarded museum (with its famed exhibit, "The Streets of Old Milwaukee"), main library, and other government buildings were located in the heart of the metropolis, a convenient half-hour drive away. The city also had a moderate zoo, with—as was the fashion then—all animals behind bars, stuck in small enclosures or cages. Years later, in one of the suburbs, the city built a very nice, modern zoo, with open-air enclosures and upgraded animal exhibits.

Cobblestone pavement, though rare, could still be found in and around Milwaukee's downtown streets. A fixture since April 1890, streetcars traveled on a network of steel rails throughout much of the city. However, largely due to the wide spread adoption of gas-powered automobiles and buses, the ridership waned greatly until that fateful day, March 2, 1958, when the service was discontinued. As fortune would have it, I rode with mother on the last trolley as it made its twilight journey into the history books.

As I recall, our family seldom ventured down to swim in Lake Michigan. The water in the lake was not that clean and it never got warm. Even during an August heat wave, with the temperature pushing triple digits, if the wind changed direction and blew off the lake, within a very short time you would need a jacket or sweater, for the temperature could drop twenty-five to thirty degrees. So, unless you were part polar bear, most folks did not linger nor play very long in the cold water.

The winters in that part of the country get so cold that, at least five times during the last 100 years, Lake Michigan has completely frozen over. During the winter of 2013-2014 it got so cold that over 92 percent of the Great Lakes were ice-covered. During that spring and summer there were even rumors of icebergs floating in Lake Superior, the most northern, deepest, and largest of the five Great Lakes.

The state of Wisconsin is blessed with many small lakes, most of which warm up nicely during the summer. So once in a while we would head to nearby, misnamed, Freeze Lake and spend some time enjoying the warm water.

Milwaukee's source of water is Lake Michigan. This was good, for even during the hot summers, when you turned on the cold water tap; the water actually came out cold. During the frigid winters, if the water would have been any colder, pieces of ice would have been coming out of the faucet.

One of my first memories of school is when I was in kindergarten (or maybe first grade). I was being taught how to read, but was not catching on. I was discouraged and angry. Of course, the reason that I failed to grasp the concept was the method used. I was not taught phonics, but the "look say" method, which had a detrimental effect upon me along with many of our nation's children.

Mother was the one who taught me how to read by wisely sounding out the words. True, her methods might have been somewhat faulty, for I still cannot spell. And years later, when I was writing my first book, I would call my "spell checker"—i.e., mom—when I just could not find the word in the dictionary, and the spell checker on my computer didn't have a clue. She got the word correct 95 percent of the time, and if not correct, she would get it close enough so that the computer's spell checker would have the word I was looking for in its list.

During my childhood, occasionally we shared the joy of canine companionship. The first dog I can recall was a good-natured, Labrador mix—short-haired, black in color, and fifty pounds of stick-chasing, rough-and-tumble fun, whom I named Dusty.

One summer day, while mom was chatting with a neighbor, a salesman decided to call upon our home. As he walked up our gravel driveway, all decked out in a black suit and tie, I am sure he thought he was about to give just another dull, routine sales presentation.

Dusty saw him approaching and, not taking too kindly to this stranger, went for him in very aggressive fashion. Her back and shoulders were all hunched up, grizzly bear style, and the fur around her neck looked like a lion's mane, with all of it standing at attention as she lunged, stiff-legged, at him. She looked mighty ferocious as she bared her teeth and growled in a frightening, menacing manner. The saliva was also a flyin' each time she barked.

I'm sure Dusty's target was eminently happy that he had remembered to bring his color-coordinated, black leather briefcase to this sales call. For he was now engaged in a curious type of dance, a rather desperate struggle to keep his briefcase between him and this jumping, wild-eyed, uncontrolled beast, who was doing her level best to see if peddlers were "aw good eat'n."

While Dusty and the salesman were kicking up stones and dust during their vigorous exercise, mother, upon hearing the commotion, looked up, and when she saw what was happening, started to laugh very hard, for she had never seen our sweet-tempered hound act this way before. She struggled to control her laughter as she tried to reassure the salesman with comforting words to this effect, "Don't worry, she doesn't bite." But the salesman was not assured, and mother's words did not erase the look of terror on his face. Their enthusiastic tango continued until mother was able to grab our spirited pooch by the collar and drag Dusty off.

I am sure that mother's boisterous laughter continued to ring in his ears throughout the remainder of the day, and our dog's ferocity must have haunted his dreams for years to come.

Besides his full-time job working for the Joseph Schlitz Brewing Company, dad held a part-time job delivering packages for the Berry Company. One day he came home with a large, black plastic bag after finishing his route. I wondered, *what could it be, a returned delivery, perhaps?* From inside the smelly bag he pulled out the largest garter snake I had ever seen. Mom freaked out and told him in no uncertain terms to "get rid of that thing right now!"

To my knowledge, garter snakes were supposed to be small and harmless, for they are not constrictors, nor do they have teeth, fangs, or poison. But this was a huge monster of a reptile; I have never seen another one even close to that size. So I thought this must be an anaconda for it was over six-feet long and about two inches thick around the middle. Being so large it also had a nasty bite—as dad found out when it bit him and drew blood! Sadly, on orders from mom, we had to grant it liberty. We released it in a tall grassy field a short distance away.

One Christmas, when I was ten, my brother, Gary, got a really neat gift: a large, realistic-looking tank that actually shot plastic shells that could fly for about 10–12 feet. Even powder that you could put into the barrel came with the tank, and when you fired the shell it looked like smoke was coming out. Of course, mother spoiled some of our fun; she wouldn't let us use the powder, for she said it was too messy.

Our Christmas tree was adorned with large, pink glass ornaments. Well, dad got down on the floor to play with

Gary and me and the tank. And wouldn't you know it, those large baubles sure made for inviting targets. By the time mother came into the room, at least three ornaments were lying in pieces on the green wool carpet, wholly destroyed by plastic shells accurately launched by the tank crew. After her arrival in the room, we three artillerymen skulked out and looked for different targets.

I do not recall seeing mother doing much housework, but I am sure she did, for our home was always clean and well organized—including my room, whether I wanted it like that or not.

With dad working two jobs to help support us, he wasn't around to do the disciplining; however, mom was well able to handle it. She used whatever was handy… her hand, a book, a board—anything that was close. And, if I happened to be in the kitchen when punishment was needed, hanging on the wall was a paddle aptly named "Heat for the Seat." There were a few times I didn't need to get a haircut for months, for mother pulled most of it out when she made me tow the line. I am glad that we didn't keep baseball bats upstairs, for if one were handy, it might have been used to my disadvantage!

Mom was also firm-handed with her grandchildren; rather than spoiling them, she regulated their behavior as effectively as she did mine.

My mother had the temperament of her brother, my Uncle Donald. Though not a man of large stature, he had a formidable bearing that put the "fear of God" in you. Though we all loved Uncle Donald, if he locked eyes with you and said the word "jump," the only thing you would say in reply would be, "Yes sir, how high?"

Mom was also stubborn, and occasionally could be downright unreasonable (I never understood why I couldn't have my own way). At times she would become angry with dad, and they would have a heated argument. During those times she didn't call him honey or sweetie. Instead, his name would slowly roll off her lips, loudly, pointedly...***R O B E R T*...!** They would always make up, but sometimes it took a few days.

During our preteen years, as each summer vacation followed its course, my brother and I would play outside for most of the day and come home only to eat, before heading out for more fun and adventures with our friends. As evening fell, mother would stand on the back porch and call her two boys home. I can still hear her cry as it echoed throughout the whole neighborhood... ***MICHAEL...GARY*...!** We could hear Mom's voice three streets over, ever so faintly, but still distinct, so I could never say, "I didn't hear you." It's a good thing we didn't live in the mountains, for loud sounds echo and can be heard a long way off. If we did, when mother called us home, every boy named Michael or Gary within a hundred miles would have showed up at our back door.

Sewing on a button was pushing the limits of her ability with needle and thread. However, when I needed patches sewn on my Boy Scout uniform (and other miscellaneous items), although it took her a long time, she did it without complaining and seemed happy to do so.

To the best of my recollection, mom didn't care for camping all that much: too many creepy-crawlies, insects that fly, and loud, mysterious noises that only occur in the deep woods after midnight. But on each outing she would always pitch in, plan the meals, then prepare the food and do whatever else was needed. She was always a welcome part of whatever we did, for we loved having her with us.

When we first started our family weekend camping trips, we would always go to Camp Luwisomo in central Wisconsin, an hour-and-a-half drive from our home. There was a good group of families that our parents got to know, and there were always good times when these folks camped with us.

On one weekend mom made chicken for lunch, but she did not cook it long enough and it was still raw when we bit into it. After she cooked it a little longer we deemed it fit for human consumption. After lunch our family took a sightseeing trip, and when we returned there were signs posted all over the camp-ground with caveats like "Raw Chicken All You Can Eat," "Raw Chicken Eat At Your Own Risk," and so forth. Their friends had heard about the raw chicken and found great humor in noting the event. My parents kept those signs for many years.

On our trips to Luwisomo we always tried to get mother's favorite spot near the outhouse, which is where mother wanted to be just in case she needed to use it in a hurry. One afternoon, when I needed to use the facilities, I saw a large beehive on the outhouse's overhang. Well, not one to let it just hang there unmolested, I found a long branch and jabbed the hive, then ran like my life depended upon it. As I looked back, there must have been hundreds, maybe thousands, of unhappy bees searching for the one who disturbed their home. About 15 minutes later, as I met mother coming back from the outhouse, she said, "Wow, there were sure a lot of bees over there!" Over the years I have often wondered, *why wasn't she stung?*

Mother, who was always somewhat claustrophobic, could not stand anything like sheets or blankets pulled right up to her neck. One cold night during a camping trip, when we were all asleep, mother woke up. Dusty was inside of my sleeping bag keeping my feet warm, and I had the bag pulled up over my head for extra warmth. I was sound asleep when I was awakened by a bright light shining in my eyes. It was mother with a flashlight, asking, "Are you all right?" She was afraid I might be suffocating because I was all covered up in my sleeping bag.

Nor did mother like heights, or driving over towering bridges. Overlooking Milwaukee's harbor stands the tied-arch span, the Daniel Hoan Memorial Bridge. One day, as we were driving over this structure, you could tell she was very uncomfortable with being up so high. As we approached its 120-foot pinnacle, Gary, in his finest southern drawl, said, "Yeah maw, thar is no air up here…" and then made noises like he couldn't breathe. I don't remember her exact reaction, but I thought the scene was hilarious.

During my junior and senior high school years, I often remember mother sitting at the kitchen table during the after-noon eating her favorite dish—macaroni covered with cooked tomatoes—while she read a Harlequin romance novel.

Wondering what she found so compelling in those books, one day I picked one up and started to read. I didn't get very far before I threw it down in disgust. "How awful," I said to myself, "how can anyone enjoy reading that stuff?" That incident not-withstanding, watching mother gain so much satisfaction from her books may have had an influence on me, for I have read many books, written four, and have hundreds of volumes in my small library.

In November of 1969 we took the Puma, our tent camper, down to Mammoth Cave, Kentucky. With over 400 miles of surveyed passageways, it is by far the world's longest known cave system.

We camped in Mammoth Cave National Park with our parents' friends, the Burgarts. They had a teenage son named John who was around my age. One morning, Gary, John, and I decided to take the three-hour tour of the cave by ourselves. It was fantastic: there were incredible, colorful formations of flow-stone; complex labyrinths; a narrow passageway appropriately called "Fat Man's Misery"; huge stalactites, stalagmites, crystal clear pools of water, and several enormous chambers. There was also the River Styx, one of the cave's semisubterranean waterways.

The cave was growing and far from inactive, for acidic water still found its way through the porous rocks. This dissolved the limestone, which allowed the cave to continue to produce new formations. As the guide led us through the cave, we saw that some of the electric wiring installed a few decades earlier was now completely covered with new flowstone one to two inches thick. Seeing that made me question the supposed millions of years of evolutionary history many geologists claim it took for all those amazing formations to form.

As we continued on the tour, my thoughts turned to the cave's ceilings and walls, which were occasionally peppered with rocks and boulders. I wondered how often those rocks rained down on those unfortunate enough to be targeted by fate. These thoughts must have been on the minds of many as our guide, seeking to calm the nerves of the tourists, declared that "No one has ever seen a rock fall anywhere in this cave." That was most reassuring—until we came to an exhibit of an unfortunate cave explorer, an adult male someone had named "Lost John." His bones were pinned down for all eternity by a large boulder that still rested upon his remains. This site was open to the public into the 1970s, when what remained of Lost John was finally interred somewhere in the cave in a secret location due to political sensitivities regarding the display of Native American remains.

After an hour or so into the tour we came to Staircase Tower in Mammoth Dome, a steel-grated structure about 80 feet in height. Inside was a lattice stairway that constituted the only way to get to the next level on the tour. When we got back to camp, Gary, John, and I told our folks all about our adventure. Then we jokingly told mother about the unusual method tour participants needed to follow to reach the higher level of the cave. As we hoped, she didn't believe us and went on the tour with dad a short time later, regardless of what we said.

Mother told us later that when she saw that staircase she ordered the guide to take her back. But he stood his ground against the stalwart force standing before him. Bravely he stated that the only thing she could do to exit the cave was climb that tower. Relenting, she closed her eyes, held onto dad, and ascended the stairway to the top. As it turned out, mother really wasn't upset with us, and with the exception of that stairway, she really did enjoy her tour of the cave.

One of the fortuitous things mother did for me was to save some of my artwork from kindergarten and the first grade. I still have it all, for I took the collection with me when we moved to the Philippines. One of these treasured items is my hand print in plaster from when I was six years old. Three years ago, when Samuel was six, I asked him to place his hand in my hand print. It was almost a perfect match to mine!

During the years my dad was alive, he and I could never really have an agreeable conversation. Our personalities just seemed to clash, and whenever we tried to discuss some random topic we would usually end up arguing. It was much different with mother. Although we did argue—sometimes very heatedly—most of the time we would both calm down and would talk for a long time afterward.

Although it was many years ago, I still remember how many times mother was there for me when I needed her the most. There were occasions when I felt worthless, that I had no friends, could do nothing right, and no one liked me. I remember sitting on the couch, at nighttime, right next to mom. She would put her arms around me and give me words of love, hope, and encouragement…these are among my most cherished memories, and they will stay with me always.

I am grateful that some of the preceding was read to mother shortly before she entered the eternal realm. For at that moment she knew, without a doubt, how much I loved and appreciated her for who she was and what she gave me.

Was she a perfect mother? No, for there is no such thing. Was she was a good mother? Heavens, yes!

As I look back, I have many regrets concerning the things I said and didn't say to mom and dad over the years. I regret that I never told my dad how much I valued the many things he did for Gary and me when we were younger, such as taking us camping, becoming a Boy Scout leader, and trying to guide us to be responsible young men.

I regret that out of necessity my wife, son, and I had to move to the Philippines and were not able to come back to visit mother during her last few years. I regret that she was deprived of not having more time with her grandson, Samuel, whom she loved so very much. I regret that I was not there at her side and that, because of my absence, the care and responsibility for most of mother's care fell largely on the shoulders of my brother and his wife, Patty. I am very grateful for their care of her.

And last of all, my greatest regret is that, when I learned mother was moved to a hospice to spend the last few days of her life, I was not able to be with her, to just sit there, hold her hand, and tell her how grateful I was for the love and kindness she showed me so many times when I did not deserve it. I regret not being able to say to her in person, for the last time, "Thank you, mother…I love you very much."

I pray that I will endeavor to live the rest of my life in a way that, when I lay dying, I will not look back upon my last few years with endless regrets, what ifs, if onlys, why didn't I do that…?

JOURNEY'S END

Death, the force that does divide
The living from the unseen side.
Life's journey that now did end,
The spirit to the living God did send.
He holds all things within His clasp,
The living, now, whose life is past.
The past with Him is not the end,
Into eternity the soul ascends.
The angels wrapped around the form
Of a loved one who is now reborn.
Born into eternal life,
Free from pain, heartache, strife.

THOUGHTS ON SELECTED POEMS AND STORIES

EPILOGUE

The poems I have written were never intended to be placed together in a book. The only reason this book came into being, I was writing to a young woman half a world away who would one day become my wife. After we started to correspond through emails, phone calls, and letters, I sent her most of the poems I had written. But I wanted to do something nice for her, so I decided to bind all the poems together into a booklet. I found an artist to do the artwork and an engraver to do the vinyl cover. The resulting product was a very nice spiral-bound book that Maribeth deeply appreciated.

THE PATH LIFE TAKES

This was the first poem I ever wrote. A friend of mine was going through some hard times, so—as a show of friendship and encouragement—I purchased a small horse figurine as a gift. But I wanted to give her a more complete gift, with a note or short letter included. So I sat down to write out a few of my thoughts, when, out of the blue, as I thought about the horse figurine, a poem started to form in my mind. An hour and a half later, my first poem was finished. Another friend read my poem and said I should try my hand at some more. I thought the first poem must have been a fluke; surely, I could not write another one. I was wrong.

RENEW EVERY DAY

Pastor Appreciation Day was coming up, and I was asked to say a few words. Instead of writing a paragraph or two, it occurred to me that maybe I could write another poem. This title became my second one.

REFLECTIONS

This poem was written for a friend, diagnosed with cancer, whom my parents had known for over forty years. My mother was very close to her. This was the poem I wrote for my friend shortly before she died.

CONTENTMENT AND PAIN

Steve grew up across the street from my brother and me. We played together and did all the things young boys do. Then we grew up, got married, and moved away (not necessarily in that order). Through the years I made sure to see Steve and Sue (his wife) at least once in a while. So when he died of a heart attack at the young age of forty-two, it was a shock. He left a wife and three young boys. I wrote this poem for Sue.

GOING NOWHERE

I was thinking of the future (not too seriously) when I asked myself a random question. Then I thought about the past and decided to write a serious poem. But I could not stay focused, nor remain in a solemn mood. *Going Nowhere* was the result.

TURMOIL AND CHOICE

A number of my poems got their start when I asked myself a question. This poem was written one morning, before I started home schooling for the day. It lays out the inadequacies I feel as a father, Christian, and teacher.

SCATTERED

This poem describes exactly how I have felt at times during the last few years.

THE LOFTY ONE

I had wanted to write about the wisdom shown by God through the beautiful things He has created. I also wanted to write about the marvelous and wonderful creatures God has made. But the poem expresses another side of God that I wasn't looking at, a side that is just as wonderful and just as beautiful. It shows His love and wisdom through the death, burial, and resurrection of Christ.

CALLING

I feel that God speaks to us in many ways, through His word (the most reliable), songs, friends, and other means. At times I believe God has spoken to me through the poems I have written. And yet I do not always like what I think He is saying. In this instance, the last few words in the poem have an ominous meaning, i.e., "You can't pray when you're dead." So, dear reader, you and I had better pray now, before our time is up.

SHE HAS

This poem was for a very special friend. I was trying to thank her for the encouragement and thoughtful words she has so generously given me.

ALONE

This poem was written late one Saturday evening. My children were with their mother for the weekend, and my plans had fallen through. I found myself alone in an empty apartment. I had no one to talk to and nowhere to go. So there, in that empty place, I put my thoughts down on paper.

IMAGINE THAT

It was the dead of night. I was ready to crawl into bed. It had been a trying day. I was lonely and depressed about the events that had brought me to this point in my life. So, as I wrote, the words took on a dark, eerie tone. After I produced about four lines, I was wondering what that negativity was. Then I started to laugh, and the gloom and despair completely vanished.

TIME

This was written after the passing of another year. As I thought of the recent past, my mind was on the truthfulness of the scripture: *"For what is your life? It is even a vapour, that appeareth for a little time, and then vanisheth away"* (James 4:14).

JURY DUTY

I wrote this while I was thinking of the probing, intrusive census questionnaire that was circulating at the time. I felt the government had no right to ask those probing questions, for most had nothing to do with how many occupants were living in a particular dwelling. I was going to send them a probing, intrusive questionnaire of my own. But, as I thought of the response I was going to craft, my anger was channeled in a different direction, and the thoughts of this whimsical tale came to mind.

www.ingramcontent.com/pod-product-compliance
Lightning Source LLC
Chambersburg PA
CBHW060453080526
44584CB00015B/1421